WILL JAMES

Lady in Boomtown: Miners and Manners on the Nevada Frontier
Mrs. Hugh Brown, 1968

The WPA Guide to 1930s Nevada
the Nevada Writers' Project of the WPA, 1940

A Kid on the Comstock: Reminiscences of a Virginia City Childhood
John Taylor Waldorf, 1970

The Story of the Mine: As Illustrated by
the Great Comstock Lode of Nevada
Charles Howard Shinn, 1896

Karnee: A Paiute Narrative
Lalla Scott, 1966

Will James: The Last Cowboy Legend
Anthony Amaral, 1980

The Legend of Grizzly Adams
California's Greatest Mountain Man
Richard H. Dillon, 1966

Curtis photo, Los Angeles

WILL JAMES

THE LAST
COWBOY LEGEND

Anthony Amaral

UNIVERSITY OF NEVADA PRESS

RENO, LAS VEGAS, LONDON

VINTAGE WEST SERIES EDITOR: ROBERT E. BLESSE

Library of Congress Cataloging in Publication Data

Amaral, Anthony A., 1930-
   Will James, the last cowboy legend / Anthony Amaral.
      p. cm.   — (Vintage West series)
   Originally published: Will James, the gilt edged cowboy. Los
Angeles : Westernlore Press, 1967.
   Includes bibliographical references.
   ISBN 0-87417-190-3 (pbk. : acid-free)
   1. James, Will, 1892-1942. 2. Authors, American—20th century—
Biography. 3. Artists—United States—Biography.   4. Cowboys—West
(U.S.)—Biography. I. Title. II. Series.
PS3519.A5298Z56   1993
813'.52—dc20   92-30235
[B]   CIP

University of Nevada Press, Reno, Nevada 89557 USA
© Anthony Amaral 1967, 1980. All rights reserved
Original version of Anthony Amaral's book Will James: The Gilt Edged Cowboy,
published by Westernlore Press in 1967. Used by permission of Westernlore Press.
Printed in the United States of America
Book design by Dave Comstock
Cover design by Kaelin Chappell
Cover photo courtesy of Special Collections Dept., University of Nevada, Reno

For my sisters—

Dolores, Beatrice, Janice

A boy's will is the wind's will,

And the thoughts of youth

are long, long thoughts.

Old Lapland Song

CONTENTS

PREFACE

WILL JAMES: It was a name which, on twenty-four self-illustrated books, scores of articles, and in the personality of the man himself, created one of the more popular and probably last cowboy legends.

As a chronicler of the idylls of cowboy life in the early twentieth century, when the image of the cowboy was at its most romantic, Will James represented and recorded a final sentimental glow.

Particularly in his famous horse story, *Smoky*, which etched one of the grandest of horse tales, and his autobiography, *Lone Cowboy*—two books time has granted status as minor classics of the West—he framed the end of the evolutionary stages of the western rider before mechanization separated him from his "fifty-fifty partner," the horse.

Thus James's writings, told in the full-flavored jargon of the cowboy, and his expressive illustrations, which encourage the eye to linger, reveal that satisfying image of a time when these men worked and played with bridle reins in their hands.

This is especially the essence of *Lone Cowboy*, in which Will James tells of being born in a covered wagon at the turn of the century in the Judith Basin of Montana. The way he tells it, his mother died when he was a year old and his father, a Texas cowman, was killed by a steer in a ranch corral three years later. At age four, according to the "lone cowboy," James was befriended by a French-Canadian trapper named Bopy. Nomadic, they traveled the isolated wilderness, with James learning the ways of the wild as well as self-reliance as he grew under the guidance of his benefactor. In his early teens, Will was again alone after Bopy drowned in a creek swift with spring-thawing water.

With saddle and packhorse, and only the knowledge Bopy had taught him, James described himself as riding the cow country trails north and south through the vast West. A lone cowboy. And his life, he writes, was part of that special vintage time of the west, of cow camps and cowboy camaraderie, of ranch life and herding cows, spring round-ups and drifting to new country when the fall gathering was done; then chasing wild horses, and coming to town for hell-raising and rodeoing. And always, there is his love for the West.

In those days, there was hardly another book or body of work which hallowed an American ideal by focusing on the West. It was a virile, spacious world of western curiosities where a man on horseback confronted living in challenging, gratifying terms. It was a world apart from the earthbound, stratified East or traditional Europe. *Lone Cowboy* made James an international celebrity, recognized as a charming exotic, *the* cowboy writer and artist who knew the smell of sage, the pungent aromas of a branding corral, and the freakish twists of a sunfishing bronc.

"Here," commented a hagiographic sketch of James in an eastern magazine, "is no lilyfingered, typewriter-tapping dude with the background of a two-week visit to Santa Fe."

As Will James was later to write: "If you follow my trail, it'll look as though a centerpede had dipped his legs in ink and then just sorta paraded on the map for a spell."

But Will James, from a fertile imagination, had invented much of himself and his deeds. Certainly, he is not the first of popular or famous personalities to be fictionalized in a self-portrait, and by today's cynical standards this might not arouse much concern. But in Will James's times, and especially in the West, he would have been humiliated and shamed for such an act had it been known.

James consequently lived under relentless emotional tension, caught between secrecy and the fear of exposure. The cloak of subterfuge and guilt intensified and, after publication of *Lone Cowboy*, slowly rotted his talents, his personal life and himself. As explained in the Sources and Acknowledgments, James contrived to hide his real identity even after his death.

Yet so magical is *Lone Cowboy* in its lyrical distillation of the West through its portrayal of one man living a grand adventure that even if it does not entirely record a real person, it is an emotionally moving and unadulterated call to nostalgia.

For James's West is the one that will always seem far better than the present. It will always be the image of a time of freedom and men on horses, a blending of fact and myth about the "Golden West" as it was and still is in the popular imagination. The illusion tugs even stronger at the feeling of loss and longing, and increasingly so, as the West continues to crowd up and become more and more citified.

And what of James's myth of himself?

He once said: "To my way of thinking, anybody with a lot of nerve is never real bad all the way."

It was this *nerve* that provided thrust and initiated turning points in his life. It drove him as a youth from his French-Canadian family in eastern Canada to the West to become a cowboy. It sustained him as he learned the craft and the art of the cowboy, while westerners critically scrutinized this achievement. And it created his fictionalized and so western past.

From this time forward, he fell prey to that illusion warned of by another artist, James B. Wyeth, who cautioned of the trap where "the personality [rather than the work] has become the product."

And, finally, the nerve which had made James destroyed him.

Still, this is not the final judgment of Will James; for above all, his nerve arose from a deep passion for horses and the American West. From this love came his writing, his art, and, in the final analysis, the true legacy of this self-made western legend.

Anthony Amaral

Carson City, Nevada
August 1979

CHAPTER ONE

OASIS, UTAH, in the fall of 1914, wasn't much more than what its name implies. With only a railroad-born array of weathered shipping pens, a small hotel, a barber shop, and a few homes, Oasis was nonetheless a welcome relief from the monotonous stretch of desert, dry lakes, and drab mountain chains for anyone driving cattle from eastern Nevada. Ely, Nevada, was also a shipping point and the logical terminus for cattle in that part of the state. Stock raisers drove their cattle to Ely. Rustlers sneaked them into Oasis.

In the barber shop of that desert town, a saddle-fatigued rider sat slumped in the barber chair. While taking a bath in a tin tub in the back room he had fallen asleep until the barber awakened him. Now he was dozing again while his face was being shaved.

At this time he was called Will James, a skinny, poorly dressed, twenty-two-year-old rider and bronc buster. He was known throughout the Nevada cow country—if not by name, by reputation—as the cowpuncher who drew pictures of bucking horses and ranch scenes which sometimes covered entire walls of ranch and bunk houses. He had another reputation as a boomer, a drifter from one outfit to another, working when he needed money and pursuing his own pleasures and interests after he had accumulated a small savings.

But bronc busting was his specialized calling. He prided himself on being one of the best in that hazardous trade and knew that he was looked up to by other riders because his horses were never spoiled or broken in spirit. No one had ever called him a bronc fighter, a derogative term for a buster of little talent.

About twenty days before his arrival in Oasis, James and another boomer of dubious reputation named Lew Hackberry (now using the alias Harry Bradberry) were working at the Jim Riordan ranch in Nye County, Nevada, when they decided to quit and drift southward. In the white sage country called Spring Valley (near the White Pine and Lincoln county line), they came upon thirty-one head of heifers and cows belonging to the Swallow brothers' ranch at Shoshone. The cattle had wandered farther south than usual, and to the quick eyes of Hackberry and James no horse tracks showed to indicate that Swallow brothers riders were aware of this drifted herd. In an apparently easy manner, the two riders decided to drive the cattle into Utah, ship them from Oasis and sell them in Denver.

During the remainder of that day they rested themselves and their horses. At dusk they started the stock moving southeast. The two boomers drove only at night and hid themselves and the stock in the hills during the day. Their circuitous route took them two hundred miles in a northeasterly direction through desert and hill country which was out of the way of traveled routes. Nights were cold and snow had obscured their way several times. Little sleep was indulged in by either man during their clandestine ten-day drive. On the ninth night they drove the cows up from Antelope Springs along the eastern edge of the Cricket Mountains in Utah. The next evening James held the cattle a few miles outside of Oasis while Hackberry rode into town and engaged a railroad car to ship the cows to Denver. They were consigned in Hackberry's name.

Between ten and eleven that night, James drove the footsore cows into the stockyards adjacent to the railroad siding. Near midnight they were loaded into the stock cars and, accompanied by Hackberry, were on their way to Denver. James was to sell the horses the next morning and purchase a ticket to Provo, Utah, where he would meet Hackberry and claim his share for the sale of the herd.

While James dozed in the barber chair early that next morning, a friend of one of the Swallow brothers heard about cattle with the Lazy GS brand having been shipped the night before. That was unusual. He followed a hunch and sent a wire to the Swallow brothers' father in Salt Lake who immediately wired the news to his sons in Shoshone.

Two men strolled into the barber shop as James was being shaved. Through his half-sleep he heard one of the men telling the barber about one lot of cattle having been shipped the past evening, and of suspicion as to the bona fide owner.

Immediately after James left the barber shop he collected the two horses from the livery and rode toward Fillmore, southeast of Oasis and away from Provo.

Meanwhile, Richard Swallow and some of his riders were gathering strays out of the mountains in the Connors Pass country when he was notified by a rider sent from the ranch that some of his cattle had appeared in Oasis. White Pine County Sheriff C. S. Crain had also been notified. Crain sent a telegram to the constable in Denver notifying him of the stolen cattle and to apprehend a Harry Bradberry on suspicion of theft. The Denver sheriff wired back that a Harry Bradley (*sic*) had sold a car of cattle in Denver for $1,471.60, and had paid his bill at the Albany Hotel.[1] There was no other trace of the man.

James, however, was apprehended by Sheriff Dougherty of Fillmore. As James and Hackberry were "well known throughout this section," according to the Ely *Record*,[2] Sheriff Crain put a tracer on James since he had ridden away from the Riordan ranch with Hackberry and both had disappeared at the same time as the cattle.

In *Lone Cowboy*,[3] James tells of stealing the cattle but has doctored the facts and promoted some fiction. Instead of being an opportunist with regard to some strayed cattle, he was compelled by revenge. As he tells it, a "home guard" (a cowman who has never left his part of the country) accused James of purposely killing a bronc because James was not able to ride the horse. James argues that the horse was one of the "crookedest outlaws in the country" and the kind that would throw himself over backwards. On the last ride James made with the bronc, the horse did just that and broke its neck.

What added to James's resentment of the home guard crew was getting into a fight with the one who accused him of killing the horse. Just as James was "getting in a few licks," some of the crew got a hold on him from behind and clamped his arms down.

"The worst part for me," says James, "was that nobody got holt of the home guard and he took advantage of that to do some pounding."

After the beating, as he recounts, James was intent on settling the score. Stealing that outfit's cattle and making them "hunt the country" for their stock seemed a just reprisal. James drove the cattle to a shipping point and, to get the cattle into the holding pen, had to take down part of the fence. But in replacing it, he inadvertently set a post upside down. The next morning, suspicion was aroused because of the inverted post, and James, being a stranger in town, was suspected and caught. James's most interesting line about this incident in *Lone Cowboy* is that he thought of escaping by using a pistol hidden in his boot. (James did carry a pistol in his boot for many years, even after he was married.) But instead, he writes, "I decided to stay and take a chance on clearing the name I was then using." Of course, he was using the name Will James.

James was apprehended about the middle of November 1914 and taken to the county jail at Ely. He admitted assisting Hackberry in the theft and said that Hackberry had all the money. James was held in jail for two months before a formal complaint was drawn and a warrant issued. This excessive length of time stemmed from the anticipation of apprehending Hackberry, for whom a hundred-dollar reward was posted on December 14.

Finally, on January 25, 1915, James was brought into Justice Court for preliminary examination. He entered a plea of not guilty through his counsel, J. M. Lockhart. Richard Swallow testified for the State.

Lockhart made an effort to shift the bulk of the stealing initiative onto Hackberry and also attempted to build a case about the cattle running wild. The judge was not impressed, especially since the cattle bore brands and earmarks. Richard Swallow testified that in a conversation with James, while the latter was in jail, James admitted that stealing the cattle seemed "a way to get some easy money."[4] James was held over on two thousand dollars bail and his trial was scheduled for early spring. He could not put up the bail and no one volunteered the bond.

With his easy manner, James made friends with jail officials during his confinement. From them he requested paper and pencil and would sketch for hours. He gave his drawings to anyone who asked for them. Many were impressed by his art as reported by the local newspaper:

Something of an Artist

Will James . . . has made many friends among county officials and others. He is a natural artist and since confinement in jail has had time to devote to drawing. His work is especially good on ranch scenes, and with proper training he would soon be able to do first class work.[5]

On April 27, after changing his plea, James was found guilty of grand larceny and sentenced to the Nevada State Prison at Carson City for a term of twelve to fifteen months.[6]

CHAPTER TWO

NEVADA'S PENITENTIARY was in the confines of what was previously the Warm Springs Stage Station, about one mile east of Carson City. From his cell James could view the flat sagebrush land spreading to the brown foothills, and above them the Sierra Nevada. Cattle and horses grazed on the flats and if it weren't for this view, he related to Mary Riordan, prison would have been intolerable for him.

Mrs. Riordan was one of James's few visitors during his confinement (James had worked at her husband's ranch previous to his ride with Hackberry). She was fond of him. He had a gay demeanor and told stories with flare. Often, he had helped her wash dishes and had done other small favors for her. In the possession of her children today are a half dozen sketches James made on the ranch which he had presented to Mrs. Riordan. Her favorite was a drawing James had sketched of a gala dance held at the ranch.

James also told her when she visited with him, "Now I know how a mustang feels when corralled."

Nothing was mentioned about the cattle incident. She did bring him drawing pencils and sketch pads, saying his talent shouldn't be wasted and encouraging him to be more serious about his art. He promised that he would.

James's first duty in prison was as a *flunky* in the mess hall, then as a woodchopper. Again because of his winning manner—easily furthered through his gifts of his drawings to any who showed interest in them—James was made a trusty. Shortly after, following an argument with the cook, he was relegated back to the woodpile.

About halfway through his term, James had another visitor named Curly Eagles. Curly ribbed James, saying that had he gone along with him and two other cowboys named Jim Campbell and Skeeter Bill, James wouldn't be in his mess right then. Neither could deny a peculiar irony to their first meeting.

Curly and Skeeter had come to Provo, Utah, from Pendleton, Oregon, with bucking stock and hopes of promoting a bronc riding show. But they went broke in two days. They decided to sell the few horses and hock their saddles for train fare to Nevada.

As Curly recalls, "We were dealing with the saddle-shop owner and were aware of this other cowboy sort of eye-feasting about the place. Didn't mean much to us. He was kind of like the rest of us, scroungy lookin', big hat on his head.

"Finally, after getting some money from the shop owner, for our saddles, this other cowboy comes over to us and introduces himself. Says his name's Bill James.

"We bought a jug, drank, and talked. 'Where're ya headed?' Bill says.

"We told him we planned catchin' mustangs around Ely, and Bill said he thought he'd head for that part of the country too. He told us he had a friend named Jim Campbell, south of Ely, who was running wild horses and that Skeeter and me could join him if we liked. It sounded okay to Skeeter and me, so we all hopped a cattle car to Ely."

Curly, Skeeter, and James met with Campbell, who demurred that he had only his own saddle and none to offer his partners.

"We improvised," says Curly. "Got some collar pads and put a surcingle around them and tied cinch rings to the sides for stirrups.

"We didn't do too well catchin' horses, though. Got a few head, but not enough to make any money. Finally, Bill gets disgusted and decides to pull out and head for where he came from. We didn't know where he meant and didn't ask. He took one of the horses he broke, and we say *adios*."

Curly, Skeeter, and Jim continued chasing mustangs for about three more weeks and accumulated a worthwhile herd. After minor gentling, it was decided to drive the herd to Hinckley, Utah (a few miles north of Oasis), where the horses could be fattened before selling.

The mustangers camped outside Hinckley for about three weeks. One morning while checking the stock, Curly noticed three head missing. He believed the mustangs might be drifting back to their Nevada range as their trail—south and then west—was the one the mustangs had been driven over to Hinckley.

"We camped out, of course, and a little after dark one night, we heard cattle being moved. They're bawlin' and we could hear some yellin' by a couple of cowboys. Well, this part of the country has always been a sort of corridor for stolen stock being pushed into Utah. It's queer alright, but none of our business.

"We caught our horses a couple of days later and took them back to Hinckley. It's there that we hear about Bill

James having pushed some stolen cattle through this country a week or so before. I knew then that it was Bill and that other jasper that Skeeter and me heard that night.

"Bill and I had a big laugh over this when I went to see him. He was a good hand with a horse. Like a lot of us, though, he tied the right stirrup to the saddle if he knew a horse was going to buck bad. Wiry fella. Saw him a couple of times later, in Hollywood, after his success."

Soaking up time in prison wasn't particularly disturbing to James. So long as he had his view from his cell window, pencil and paper, and someone willing to listen to him tell stories, James felt little discomfort while confined. During the last few months of his term, he became a trusty again, this time outside the walls working with the prison stock.

James was paroled on April 11, 1916, one month earlier than the scheduled end of his sentence. He stayed in Carson City for a few days and, through a local bartender, heard that a rancher from Smith Valley was in town looking for some good help. James searched out the rancher, Bill Dressler of the Plymouth Land and Stock Company, but was forewarned by Dressler that the job wasn't riding. What Dressler needed was a milker.

"Can you milk?" Dressler asked.

"Sure," answered James.

James wasn't playing square. He knew nothing about milking, and deemed working for any outfit that drank milk or "pumped" cows as bad as being a sheepherder. But he was broke, although ten dollars in "gate money," as he called it, was due him from the prison.

At Smith Valley he was assigned twenty-five cows that had to be milked twice a day.

"Christ!" recalls Jeff Rice, "he didn't know anything about milking a cow. After two days, his hands began to swell."

Jeff had met James once before, around Great Falls, Montana. Both of them were then about eighteen years old, drifting and riding the bronc string at various ranches.

"While in Montana," says Rice, "we split a bottle between us until we went our separate ways."

Jeff choked down a laugh when James told him he would be milking cows. James caught Jeff's smile and said, "I can't blame ya, Jeff. I might as well de-horn my boots."

James had milked the cows twice a day for two weeks when a rider from the Rickey outfit out of Bridgeport, California, stopped by. James asked if any riding jobs were available and was told there were some broncs needing a rider, if he were interested. James collected what pay was due him and proceeded to Bridgeport.

The broncs were corralled at a line camp near Topaz, the winter range for the Rickey ranch. They were a husky bunch that had been caught in Nevada. For about two weeks, James rode and gentled six of the broncs. One, though, a mature stallion, fought stubbornly and had to be thrown to have a hackamore placed on his head. While another rider was helping James tie down the stallion, the bronc lashed out with a rear leg, striking James in the jaw and knocking him out immediately. His teeth had been in bad condition and the blow from the stud's hoof loosened and split most of them on the left side of his jaw.

James was laid up for a few days, but the pain did not subside. Most of the riders agreed he would have to see a dentist. That prospect seemed inevitable even to James, who disliked any sort of doctor. He had little money but realizing he could wait no longer, he turned in his time and decided to go to Los Angeles.

A few days before he scheduled himself to leave, a rider with a packhorse trailing behind came to the ranch to spend the night. He was Fred Conradt of Reno, another horsebreaker with whom James had occasionally ridden in Nevada. Fred tried to persuade James to come with him to Reno where he was on his way to do some rodeoing. He said he'd be staying with his family there and offered James a free roost while being treated by a Reno dentist. Even though James liked the idea he declined, feeling that Los Angeles could offer a better specialist to take care of his aching teeth.

Before Fred rode out of camp the next morning, he told James to look him up whenever he passed through Reno. "Got some sisters fulla hell," he added.

In Los Angeles, James took a room at a small hotel while he scouted for a dentist he could afford. He found one located near the section that was called Edendale. He also found the Jones stable, "a little cow country," he later wrote, which supplied horses, buggies, wagons, oxen, and stuntmen for the fledgling motion picture industry. James lingered around the stable daily and made acquaintances. In a short time, he was riding and stunting pell-mell in front of the cameras.

James has related his early Hollywood days in both *Lone Cowboy* and *Drifting Cowboy* with differing accounts. But he does make an interesting story about doubling for cowboy stars, jumping horses off twenty-foot cliffs, throwing horses over backwards in the eye of the camera, and "meeting all those show girls—some nice ones, too—of all styles from running to draft types."

Most of the cowboys at the Jones stable were refugees from the range, enticed to come to Hollywood to lend authenticity to the westerns which were giving the mute cameras something to say through action films. Hollywood was still an unorganized and not fully awake industry. Any cowboy able to ride a horse could earn five dollars a day just galloping a horse, and possibly a twenty-dollar bonus if he pulled a stunt that satisfied the director. The cowboy riders and stuntmen were clannish and as rough and hard drinking a bunch of cowboys as has ever gathered anywhere. The Jones stable was their headquarters and here they waited for calls from the studios. Jones, however, wasn't running any free rent hangout for the cowboys. He kept them working at building wagons, repairing harness, cleaning tack, and breaking horses while they waited.

"That James kid," remembers Clarence Jones, "was the laziest of the bunch, unless he was on top of a horse. One reason I remember him, and hundreds of cowboys have floated through here in the past fifty years, was because of his drawings. For a while they were tacked all over the place. I only have one now, dated 1916. After James left here, his pictures began to disappear from the barns and sleeping quarters, so I grabbed the one I considered his best."

James rode for the Thomas Ince Studios which produced many western pictures, and he wrote with considerable detail about his doubling and stunting for "that doggoned pink leading man in *Six Guns and Rope*." The director, according to James, liked his appearance and apparently there might have been a future for him as a Western cinema hero. But at the moment, with a few dollars in his pocket, his dental work finished, and the rainy season quieting the cameras and the acting work, James was becoming anxious for the cow country. There the snow patches were trickling to an end and the grass shoots were spreading patches of green. "Little white faces were coming into the world, and remudas were being run in from winter range in preparation for the spring round-up." Nostalgia was stirring James.

He took the train to Tonopah, Nevada. On and off since about 1910 James had worked for most of the cattle ranches in the Tonopah area. In fact, the few outfits that James does describe by name or brand in his first stories center in the Tonopah and eastern Nevada country.

With a horse under him, James rode toward the Stone Cabin Valley, east of Tonopah, where local ranches converged for spring and fall round-ups. The Salsbury outfit provided James a job and for two months he worked at the chores of herding strays from out of the Monitor Forest Range and down to the desert "cutting grounds" for branding and castrating.

About June, James quit and decided to drift north. At the Barley Creek ranch in the Monitor Valley, owned by Joseph Nay, James was invited to stay the night. He put his saddle and pack horse into a corral and helped Joe Nay butcher hogs. Encouraged by the Nay family, who immediately liked his subtle humor and his stories about Hollywood, James stayed ten days.

Olephia Nay[7] was thirteen at the time and remembers James vividly since she also had an interest in art. In the evening she and James would sketch, and James would advise her about anatomy and positions of horses while bucking and running.

Joe Nay thought James was loco to be just a rider when he could become an artist and "pack in better wages." James mentioned that he would like to be an artist "like the one [Charlie Russell] in Montana." This was a wish that James had frequently made to himself, but he took his art more seriously in times of depression and discouragement than in times when all was going well. He was still young and liked to drift, "to see the country." Traipsing was easy, and if he had money and a couple of horses his mind slipped into the lackadaisical attitude he preferred. The desire to be an artist was within him, but he wasn't yet moved to devote himself to art full-time.

James mounted his horse, left the Nay ranch, and rode along the now-forgotten stock trails to Beowawe in the cattle country around Elko. This part of northern Nevada was one of James's favorites. A vast open country where cattle mingled with antelope, it had more than the vestiges of the open range days and was, in fact, one of the last pockets of the range country that still had no branding corrals or chutes, or fences cutting across the land. In his letters to Olephia (James promised that he would comment and "check over" her drawings if she would send them to him) he had said that he would stay in Beowawe. However, he apparently sold his horses and continued north by train until he arrived in Malta in northeastern Montana. A job was available at the Circle Dot ranch winter-feeding cows and breaking a few broncs. James remained there the entire winter.

In the spring, with a good part of his pay saved from virtual hibernation, he went south to Tuscarora about seventy miles north of Elko. For three months he worked on the Old Spanish ranch. In July, James decided to work another winter in Montana. He sold his horses and started north, going first, however, to Calgary, Canada.

Lloyd Garrison, a Canadian cowpuncher, was home on leave in August from the Canadian Army. At Calgary he joined with some of the boys, among whom was James. Garrison had met him once before, around 1914, in Medicine Hat and believed James had come up from Malta over the wild horse trail.

James told Garrison at this second meeting that "things were going bad for him and that he was going back over the line to join the army." Garrison goes on to say:

"Well, after Bill left, I got with Bob Stadley, Calgary Red, and Sleepy Eperson, and we were going to make a few of the shows or stampedes. We were traveling in Red's old Model T Ford. First show we hit was at Taber, and we run into Bill. So right now, he comes with us. I recall he drew bucking horses and cowboys all over the Ford with colored crayons. We made the Taber show—Bill put on a good ride—then on to

Moose Jaw, the Big Gap out of Hardisty, and back to Winni-
fred, then to Medicine Hat. All this before I reported back to
the Army. I recall the last night in Medicine Hat, when we
put on a show in the street. Calgary Red did some rope spinning, and Bill did the announcin'. We all did a lot of singin',
and we all drank too much.''

Garrison left the next morning and the rest of the cowboys
broke up shortly afterward.

James was out of sight that winter and possibly did return
to the Montana country to punch cows from a hay wagon, as
he had the past winter. By spring of 1918, however, he was in
serious trouble with the draft board who could not locate
him. Their letters had followed him, but he always was ahead
of them.In early May James rode into Winnemucca, Nevada,
to check at the local draft board about his status. An official
told him he was about to be sought throughout the country as
a draft dodger. On May 20, 1918, he was inducted and assigned to Headquarters Company, 21st Infantry, and sent to
Camp Kearny, California, Less than a year later, in February,
James was honorably discharged with the rank of private.

CHAPTER THREE

SOMETIME BETWEEN 1917 and 1919 James purposely went to Great Falls, Montana, to see the artist Charles Russell. Typically, James does not mention Russell by name in *Lone Cowboy*, but refers to him as "that artist which all the cowboys knowed or heard of . . . I'd been packing some postcards which had been printed from his work."

It may have been one of James's depressed moods that spurred him to see Russell, to get an evaluation of his own art work from one who "was making a lot of money at that game."

In his free-roaming days, James was always cocky about his talents. His self-esteem came from being a cowboy and an artist, in this order, and it would be some years to come before he would realize that art, like living, is best when it is simple, and simplicity in either, he was to learn, is difficult to achieve. His only art critics had been cowboys and other well-meaning encouragers whose opinions were hardly those of experts. James's sketches at this time were cumbersome with details that distracted from the main action, and his horses were depicted in exaggerated ''wild west'' poses. He still had some learning to do.

When James came to the Russell house he felt he had arrived as an artist and that Russell would recognize his talent and provide the ropes for him to hoist himself to fame. Nancy Russell answered the door knock and invited him to sit in the parlor while she went to the studio to announce him. A minute later she returned and escorted him to the studio.

Of Russell, James wrote: ''The whole map of the cow country was on his face. I could see at a glance that he'd squinted over many herds of cattle and that he was all cowboy as well as artist.''[8]

What James didn't expect was the curt and hollow encouragement he received from Russell.

Russell was painting when James silently walked into the studio filled with canvases, smells of pigment, and an array of western artifacts hanging over chairs and from wall pegs. He stood there a few minutes, feeling like an awkward intruder. Sitting in a corner was Joe DeYong, an artist and protege of Russell's. (The Russells would gladly have adopted Joe DeYong as a youth but, according to nephew Austin Russell, Joe had ''a couple of practicing parents of his own who seemed quite fond of him.''[9])

Russell looked up at James, uttered a salutaton in the form of a grunt, then focused his attentions back to the canvas in front of him. The painting had bogged down, and he sat in one of his deeply absorbed moods, lost almost completely from anything and anybody around him. It was an engrossment that only a few, such as Nancy and Joe, understood.

James asked Russell about his problem with the painting to crack the impersonal air. Russell mumbled an answer. Annoyed, James held out a batch of his drawings which Russell took with an outstretched hand without looking at James. Russell laid them on his lap and continued working on his picture. Finally he put his paint brush down and shuffled through James's drawings "as if they were cards, getting ready to play stud poker and deal out a hand, and just as quick as he shuffled 'em and while I was waiting for surprised remarks, my deck of drawings was handed back to me, and he went to work on his picture again, just as though I still wasn't around and like he'd never seen them pictures of mine."[10]

James asked Russell what he thought of them.

"Good," Russell answered reticently.

James then asked where he could sell them. Russell told him to scatter them around saloons. "Somebody might buy them."

James said a polite goodbye and left.

"I sensed," related Joe DeYong in later years, "that Bill assumed he received something in the nature of a brush-off and I followed him outside to explain the matter. However, his drawing and description of the meeting in *Lone Cowboy* indicated that he still believed that Charlie's attitude was a matter of personal indifference."

Russell's manner cast a pall over James's enthusiasm. But it was only a shadow of discouragement, and was soon overcome by the memory of the craftsmanship James had seen in Russell's canvases. James felt an urge to paint too and admitted in later years that his visit to the Russell studio made him conscious that his own work was only mediocre, that even natural talent needed practice and study. With this urge came stirrings of a desire for a studio of his own where he could paint, somewhere in the hills, close to the land and horses and cattle.

In May 1919 James came to Reno to visit with Fred Conradt. He found Fred and another cowboy friend named

Elmer Freel. Reno became the last location in James's gypsy ramblings over the West. Here, he found a close kinship with Fred and Elmer, and together they became a fun-loving, rowdy, lazy trio. They called themselves the one-elevens (the 111s) and made a pact that whoever of the three would someday own a ranch, would share it with the other two.[11] Together they broke horses, entered bronc contests held at the outlying ranches, and were generally inseparable. Most of the time they were broke, although James occasionally earned one to five dollars sketching advertising posters for local merchants. He was paid twenty dollars by fairground officials to illustrate posters and a souvenir program for the First Annual Nevada Round-Up Rodeo held in Reno in July 1920.

When he first came to Reno, he slept in the alfalfa fields and later in a stall at the fairgrounds. Fred sneaked James's clothes in with his own laundry which his sisters washed. They became wise to the stunt but said nothing, for James had become well liked by Fred's mother.

Fred's family consisted of his parents, four other brothers, and seven sisters. To Alice, the third youngest, James took an immediate liking. Alice was then about fifteen—tall, and strikingly attractive. But she couldn't care less about a cowboy. Her parents, Edward and Mary, had emigrated from Germany to Hawaii where her father hoped he could find use for his building trade. Hawaii, however, was developing too slowly, and so the father moved his family to Oklahoma. Shortly afterward, the family again moved, this time to San Francisco, and then to Sacramento where he developed a sawmill business. Alice was born in Sacramento in 1904. When she was about three, her family moved permanently to Reno.

James ate with the Conradts frequently. He told stories of his life as an orphan and of his tramping all around the country. James would often direct his comments to Alice, but she ignored his attentions. To her, James wasn't much different from most cowboys—shiftless—and just another of Fred's buddies who all seemed to be quite the same and without ambition. While Alice was willing to be impersonal to James, her father took an immediate dislike to him. James was too rowdy and what was more, he told Alice, James seemed the type that would "have a record."

Although James poured out to the Conradts his desire of someday being an artist, he still wasted too much time as a fun-lover. He had spells of studying magazine illustrations, sketching horses out in the pastures, or studying animal anatomy books. These would last a week or two until Fred or Elmer suggested some adventure to pursue, usually a bronc contest. Yet, even these assertive moments at art showed James that he had a style of his own and that it came to a polish with even a short time of thoughtful study. He was nearing the time now when a critic would exclaim that James's horses looked as though "they were jumping right out of the page."

If James was too much of a fun-lover to give lengthy attention to art, as Alice had once hinted to him, it made little difference at the time. For actually, it was this fun-seeking attitude that brought James to a critical point in his life.

It was one of those summer days, hot and severe on three cowboys who had whooped it up at a Reno club the night before. James, Elmer, and Fred were loafing on the back porch of the Conradt house tossing about ideas on what they should do. Fred perked up with the thought of using his three broncs to put on local bucking horse shows and then take up a collection.

Alice thought the idea silly when it was explained at the supper table that night. But the one-elevens were restless and wanted something to do other than roaming around the Reno clubs. When Alice's father suggested they get themselves jobs, they completely passed over that idea.

James had two important horses in his life: Smoky, the blue roan that would inspire him to write the classic book of that name, and Happy, a black bronc that finished James as a bucking horse rider and brought him closer to Alice and art.

Two of Fred's top broncs were named Hell-Morgan and Soleray. The one-elevens bantered over who was to get which horse. James shied away from Hell-Morgan. That horse had been used in the Reno rodeo a few months before and done a fair job of tossing his riders. James hinted to his partners that he was avoiding any more rough horses. So he selected Happy, while Fred drew Hell-Morgan and Elmer got Soleray.

James and Elmer decided to ride their horses and get the feel of them before trailing them to likely areas where they could gather an audience. With them went Fred's brother, Gus, to take some pictures to be used on a publicity poster.

Fred ran the horses into the corral. James roped Happy and started to throw his saddle on the horse. When he described this saddle years later, he admitted he knew better than to use a roping type which was hardly adequate for bronc riding.

"The boys," said James, "used to kid me about the cantle, saying all it was good for was to keep a feller from setting down."[12]

Actually it wasn't the cantle that caused him some uneasiness, but the pair of twenty-six-inch tapaderos that hung from the stirrups. James thought about removing them before saddling Happy, but the hunch wasn't strong enough. Besides, Fred said that Happy was only an average bucking horse and considered him easy pickings for James. What Fred and James failed to consider was that Happy hadn't been ridden for nearly three months—a lot of time to "stack up on orneriness."

While Fred eared Happy down, James slipped into the saddle and settled himself firmly. He indicated to Fred to let go of the hold on Happy's ears. Immediately, the horse leaped into a series of hard, pile-driving jolts. James quickly caught the rhythm of Happy's tactics and figured that Happy would be a breeze to ride.

Maybe Happy sensed that overconfident attitude, for at that moment the horse came to a shuffling stop and bowed his neck. Instead of making a hard, forward jump as James expected, Happy went up and whirled in a backward spin, throwing James's rhythm and timing. Happy whirled again and James lost his left stirrup. He reached for the saddlehorn while his foot fished for the stirrup which the tapadero was swinging like a kite.

James knew he was putting on a bum ride, but he stuck to Happy as best he could. The horse went from hard jolts to easy crow hops and it felt to James that Happy was about ready to run. Heavy timber lay ahead, and James decided this was as good a time as any to hop off, just in case Happy planned to clear the timber out of his way. James braced himself, preparing to swing his right leg over the saddle. Just as he began to ease off, he glimpsed railroad tracks glinting light from the sun. He changed his mind and started to settle back in the saddle until after Happy had detoured away from the tracks. But it was too late. While James was still half out of the saddle, Happy suddenly leaped into the pile-driving part of his repertoire. The third jolt chucked James. He landed between the tracks with his head hitting one of the rails.

A doctor was called. During the thirty minutes James was unconscious, his torn scalp was temporarily bandaged. The doctor told Fred that further treatment was needed at the hospital. After James slowly regained consciousness, Fred and Elmer helped him to stand. While they steadied him, James began to sing, "Oh bury me not on the lone prairie. . ." There was a broad, silly grin on his face, and one of the spectators who had gathered commented: "He's out of his head."

James looked to the man and answered, "You'd be out of your head too if you tried to bend a railroad track with it."

CHAPTER FOUR

A CONCUSSION and twenty-two stitches in his scalp forced James to rest in bed for about two weeks. After two days in the hospital, however, he was released as Fred offered his room to James for the remainder of his convalescence.

The accident, which could easily have been fatal, unsettled James and started him thinking about his future. He was now twenty-seven, with nothing to show but a lot of drifting and tomfoolery.

While he stayed in bed, sketching for hours, he continued in self-reflection. In the past, James had been bone-broken and busted as a bronc string rider. If he continued this activity, he realized, the broncs would get the best of him. He was acquainted with a number of old-timers who were once agile, top buckaroos like himself. While some were lucky and had found a pet position on some ranch where they could spend the rest of their lives, far too many were lost souls, drinking heavily and merely existing instead of living.

Alice spent considerable time in conversation with James while he rested in the Conradt house. Although she hadn't particularly cared for James when she first met him and had ignored his flirtations, he seemed more gentle and pleasant since his accident. They talked about horses and, especially, his hopes to study art. Alice, just as James wished, was an attentive listener. The way was opened for him to talk more freely about himself.

Alice caught her first glimmer of the romantic sentiment James held for the West. He bemoaned the way the country had changed—railroads, fences, sheep and foreigners to herd them, and engine power that was beginning to sweep the horse off farms and ranches. He talked in detail about being an orphan, losing Bopy, never having a home, and being a drifting cowboy all of his life.

She sensed in his melancholy memories a man sensitive and sentimental, and beyond the cowboy bravado he acted with Fred and Elmer and other cowboys.

Although his sensitivity and sentimentality when he talked about the West was true enough, there is little doubt that James also used the fiction of his early past as a dramatic ploy to gain sympathy and attention from Alice.

One of his frequent and favored talks with her was what she called his "log cabin talk." It crops up in James's writings every so often with only the slightest provocation. When he became moody, he would talk about having a cabin somewhere in the pines, with a brook running by, a few head of horses about the place, and a studio where he could draw and even try painting.

In the weeks during James's convalescence, Alice found herself becoming as anxious for his aspirations as he seemed to be. She wanted to be part of them and of the man for whom she was feeling an ever-closer association. When at last he talked specifically about going to an art school in San Francisco, Alice agreed and told him, "By all means, stop riding bucking horses."

Alice's mother had also become fond of James and encouraged Alice to marry him. Alice's father, however, was still cool to him. Without voicing his opinion, his attitude reflected that he didn't care for the attentions James and Alice were exchanging. He did tell his wife that Alice was too young even to think about a serious courtship with a man over ten years her senior. And besides, James hadn't really shown himself to be anything more than a loafing cowboy.

James and Alice realized that art school was the best move he could make now. Not only for himself, but to show Alice's father that he, James, was more reliable and ambitious than Conradt believed.

In August 1919, James arranged to go to San Francisco and enroll in the California School of Fine Arts. He also planned to visit the editors of *Sunset* magazine in San Francisco which, at the time, was editorially favorable to the type of subjects his art portrayed.

James hocked his saddle for train fare. Before boarding the train, Fred and Elmer handed James the few dollars they had. James refused, but Fred insisted, "Hell, take it. The clubs would get it anyhow."

In September, James registered for evening classes in art school and took a small apartment on Howard Street. About the same time, he found a convenient job as usher in a movie theater where he worked the matinee shift. He settled into a routine of morning art practice, a job in the afternoon, and school in the evening. Shortly thereafter, and either through the school or by his own connections, James created advertising posters for the Bear Furniture Company and one for the Levi-Strauss Company, makers of denim pants. The latter poster showed two bear cubs, each on a leg of the pants, trying to pull them apart.

While these assignments were encouraging to James, school was becoming an ordeal. The discipline of still-life studies and the repetition of practice became too stilted and somber for his crisp, free style. His interest waned, and one evening the instructor noticed his lack of interest in a nude model. He asked James why he was not sketching. James answered, "If I'm to draw udders, I'd rather draw them on cows than on nice ladies."[13]

Another evening, a guest of the instructor, Lee Rice, visited to view and comment on the students' work. Rice, a noted artist and writer for horse magazines, previously had been a *vaquero* with considerable experience on California ranches. Looking over the class, his eyes halted on the bow-legged fellow wearing cowboy boots. Rice walked to James's desk and peered over his shoulder. The class was sketching a human figure. Rice recalls James's efforts were something of an insult to the female model. But along the margins of his sketchbook were small drawings of cowboys riding bucking horses. Rice was also wearing the symbol of his breed— boots—and immediately the two struck a natural accord as fellow travelers of the range country.

They became friendly and saw each other frequently. After class, James and Rice would usually meet in some small restaurant to talk art, Charlie Russell, and Remington, and to retell stories of their experiences as cowboys.

Rice was acquainted with Maynard Dixon, an excellent artist and popular illustrator, and introduced James to him.

Unlike Russell in his meeting with James, Dixon was outgoing, friendly, and generous with encouraging advice that may have inspired another turning point in James's life. Dixon studied the cow country sketches James had brought with him. He also studied James's technique from a bucking horse James had sketched for him. Afterwards, Dixon advised him to quit art school. The instructional methods of the school, with its emphasis on preliminary sketching, he felt might ruin rather than help what Dixon considered James's natural gift. Dixon noticed, too, that James did nothing that was either academic or conventional in his techniques. Instead, he drew directly, without preliminary sketching, and with immediate results in his mind. Thus James was able to put a complete idea on paper in a matter of minutes.

Art school could probably have helped James in drawing human figures (necks are notoriously absent from his), but the risk was that it might have ruined his unique free style. He dropped out of art school shortly thereafter.

Dixon and James became steady companions and, along with Rice, rode horseback together in the nearby hills. Dixon's advice and criticism helped build James's confidence. Through this bolstering, he was now eager to approach the *Sunset* editorial office.

He probably would have been turned down in his request to see Joseph Henry Jackson, then an assistant editor, had he not presented a letter of introduction from a mining friend of Jackson's whom James had met in the hospital after Happy had dumped him. The miner, also a western buff, had a bed next to him and was impressed with his sketches. In any case, his letter did get James into Jackson's office. But Jackson was not too impressed with James's portfolio.

"We couldn't use such drawings as these," James reports Jackson as saying. "They would have to be a lot better. Come around again some other time."

"When?" James asked.

"Oh, in a few months or so, when you have something else to show me."

James later learned that Jackson liked his style and felt that if James was really interested in art and in illustrating for the magazine, he would return showing improvement through greater effort.

Having been shunned by Jackson and losing any hope for immediately selling his sketches, James turned his thoughts momentarily to another job. He had quit the movie house following his acquaintance with Rice and Dixon. The only job listing requiring no experience was a riveter's helper on the dry docks in the shipyards. In his letters to Alice, James complained about how discouraging it was to work so close to people that his eyes could hardly stretch themselves for a healthy look to a horizon. "I don't like steel and soot," he wrote. "I like flesh and dust."

Before the letter even arrived in Reno, James had quit the job. He'd been feeling groggy and dizzy, and at first he thought the dizziness was caused by the height of the scaffolds. But then pain whirled in his head. James feared he might fall and quit the day after he had started.

That evening in his room the pain became severe. He tossed for awhile and then slept. When he awoke, he felt something wrong with his eyes. A burning sensation was causing them to water profusely. He turned on the light switch, but was jolted by a sense of darkness.

Presumably, the head injury he had sustained when Happy bucked him onto the railroad track had become agitated through the riveting vibrations, causing temporary blindness. After several unnerving hours of blurred vision, the pain subsided and his sight returned.

Once over that shock, James completed a series of cow country sketches to offer to *Sunset* magazine. He returned to Jackson's office about a month after his first visit. Jackson thumbed through the sketches depicting tragic and comic vignettes of animals on the range. He bought two for twenty-five dollars each and promised to buy others of the series once James made a few changes.

One-Man Horse, which James says was a portrait of himself and his horse Smoky, appeared full page in the January 1920 issue of *Sunset*. From then on, with the exception of about a year, James's work would appear in print the rest of his life.

CHAPTER FIVE

INITIAL SUCCESS had come relatively easy to James. If this is not a tribute to the proverbial persistence which characterizes many artists and writers before receiving wide acceptance, then definitely it is a tribute to James's natural talent which was developing a sparkling quality all its own.

Jackson took personal pride in being the first editor to recognize James's art, and when James was nationally known a few years later, Jackson wrote in his "Across the Editor's Desk":[14]

"To find, develop and bring out new talent is the favorite sport of every editorial office. Rare talent is so scarce that its discovery causes as much joy around the desk as the arrival of Santa Claus in a house full of children. Therefore, Will James with his half-dozen crude but vivid drawings was received with open arms . . .

"This lean youngster with the tang of the sagebrush still

clinging to him made good because he carried into his drawings—and into his writing—the unadulterated flavor of the desert and mountain, because the subtle essence of that spiritual attitude which we call the Far West pervaded everything he did.

"We are proud of Will James and we are patting ourselves on the back . . . for having roped, tied and broken him for the role in the arena of arts and letters."

Virtually every month *Sunset* featured a full-page James sketch, usually with an editor's note such as, "The artist has had no training in art, but he has remarkable natural talent from years of life as a cowboy and a sympathetic knowledge of the actors in such a tragedy."

James sold a batch of drawings at a time with a simple title under each.

His more popular drawings with *Sunset* readers were: "Mothers," a cow and a bear, each with her young, meeting with startled expressions on a mountain trail; "Friend in Disguise," a sketch of a lion ready to attack a horse, but the horse is saved from attack by shying from a snake rattling in the brush; and the popular "Keno, the Cowhorse," a series of nine sketches depicting the life of a cow pony.

All his pictures told a simple story about the ways of animals and are generous evidence of an observing eye. Along with his own sketches, Jackson assigned James to illustrate a series of range poems by E. C. Lincoln. But when James had to slant his sketches to the thought of another writer they never quite had the feel that he conveyed in his own.

Flushed with pride from the acceptance of his work and a steady income for a refreshing change, James plunged wholeheartedly into art. He moved to Sausalito to be with the local art colony, and, seemingly, he tried to change his breed and brush shoulders with those aspirants to the art world. But they revolted him because of what he felt was the artificial atmosphere they created for themselves. From then on, James shied away from academic art and artists, and none of the old masters would mean anything to him. Only Russell, and to a lesser degree Remington, were masters to him, and James studied them diligently.

In April 1920, James wrote Russell and sent a sketch with his letter asking advice and criticism. Russell replied:[15]

May 12, 1920

Hello Will James:

I got your letter and sketch and from it and other worke I have seen of yours in Sunset I know you have felt a horse under you. Nobody can tell you how to draw a horse ore cow.

I never got to be a bronk rider but in my youthful days wanted to be and while that want lasted I had a fine chance to study hoss enatimy from under and over . . . the under was the view a taripan gits. The over while I hovered ont the end of a Macarty rope was like the eagle sees grand but dam scary for folks without wings.

James, you say you havnt used color much dont be afraid of paint I think its easier than eather pen ore pensol

I was down in Cal this winter and saw some fine ground for cow pictures rolling country green with patches of poppies and live oak mountain ranges with white peaks that streach away to no where I have never seen this kind of country used in cow pictures

Why dont you try it . . .

James as I said before use paint but dont get smeary let sombody else do that keep on making real men and cows of corse the real artistick may never know you but nature loving regular men will and thair is more of the last kind in this old world an thair the kind you want to shake hands with . . .

With best wishes to yourself and any who know me

Yours

C. M. Russell

In June 1920, Alice and her mother went to Sausalito to visit Alice's sister, Annie. As a favor to Alice, particularly after James had written to her about his head pain and near blindness, Annie occasionally telephoned or visited with James. In her last letter to Alice she wrote that James was lonely and spent most of his time alone in his cottage.

James was overjoyed when Alice arrived. For the first few hours he did nothing but talk of art, Jackson, and future plans. It was all repetition of what he had written in his letter. But for the first time he spoke of marriage, and also about wanting to go back to Nevada. He didn't like the city. "Concrete don't set with my soles like the desert does," he told her.

James did come back the month following the visit of Alice and her mother. One month later, on July 7, 1920, Alice and James were married in Reno. She was sixteen and he twenty-eight. A honeymoon was waived for the time since money was scarce.

They returned to Sausalito where James finished a set of drawings for *Sunset*. Soon after, *Sunset* informed him that it had a substantial backlog of his drawings and that those would be all it could use for some time. Although an illustrating assignment came from the magazine office now and then, it was more than apparent that he and Alice would soon be out of money unless he could persuade other magazines to use his work.

James studied the East Coast magazines more closely. As always, he was annoyed at the obvious lack of first-hand knowledge on the part of their western story illustrators. He felt certain that if once he could gain the favor of one magazine, others would turn to him. He told Alice that success with the eastern publishers could mean a place of their own, off by themselves with horses, cattle, and a studio for his work.

He assembled a portfolio of sketches and cover ideas for a western pulp publishing chain and sent them to New York. They were all promptly returned. He tried two other eastern magazines, and again his portfolio was sent back. His mood began to change to a pensive meditation that confused Alice in her efforts to help him. He didn't want any help, but only to be left alone.

Discouraged, James wanted to go back to Nevada and cowboy work. It was a rationalization, a return to something in which he felt more secure. Alice offered little advice or opinion in countering James's motives and contemplated moves. In the first few years of their marriage, she believed all he told her and abided by whatever he decided as being best for both of them. Still, she was astute enough to recognize some weaknesses in his temperament, but also as quickly learned not to confront James with them. Once, in Sausalito, she had suggested that he write about Bopy and his travels with the French trapper. James replied caustically that the idea was asinine. He was an artist, he said, and not a writer.

In the meantime, James had written to a rancher in Arizona who Elmer Freel said might be looking for some help at one of his line camps. James specified to the rancher that broncs were out of his working line. To James's surprise, the rancher replied that all he needed was someone to live at a line camp where horses and cattle on the range came for water.

Mostly, it was a stock-watching job, checking water, setting out salt, and doctoring animals that needed attention.

The job seemed ideal to James and Alice, one where he obviously could still devote time to his art. James wrote a letter of acceptance.

From Sausalito they went to Reno for a brief visit with Alice's family and then by train to Arizona. Near the middle of the night outside Kingman, James and Alice, according to the rancher's instructions, had the brakeman stop the train at the water tank. Close by was the small ranch house of another ranch employee, where James was to announce himself.

James and Alice waited until the train pulled away before starting toward a pale light glowing from the ranch house about a quarter of a mile away. After trekking only a few minutes through the darkness, stumbling through unseen cactus and desert brush which tripped them and pulled at their clothes and bulky luggage, James started to mumble curses. Alice was about to join in with a protest of her own when the absurdity of it all caused her to start giggling.

James stopped and turned to look at her. He began laughing himself, seeing her awkwardly lugging two suitcases.

At the ranch house they were greeted by an elderly male employee who fed them and was willing to talk the night away. James insisted that he and Alice were tired and wanted to go to bed. The next morning the host drove James and Alice to the line camp heavily stocked with food and a letter of instructions.

The line camp was a new experience for Alice. Although she had grown up in a desert state, she had always lived within city limits. Now, fifteen miles from anywhere, and with all sorts of shy creatures crawling along the ground and startling her, she was frightened. James was completely at ease. He told her about the snakes, the Gila monsters, and the spiders and scorpions that inhabit the Arizona country. She cried one time and accused him of trying to frighten her.

But he informed her that the only way she could protect herself was to understand the nature of the creatures and, if he should be away, to know how to care for herself if bitten.

He also attempted to teach her how to shoot a pistol. After a few sessions marked without improvement in Alice's marksmanship, he suggested that she had best try and hide rather than "shoot it out."

Their billet was a large one-room cabin with a stove, small bed, bench chairs, and outside toilet. One corner of the cabin held their cache of flour, sugar, dried fruit, and canned goods. Cooking was no problem to Alice as she had learned early in her life how to prepare tasty meals with a minimum selection of foods.

Twice a day, cattle and horses would wander into the camp for water from the spring, and James inspected them at every visit. Other times, after the necessary chores of getting firewood or butchering a calf (James jerked most of the meat), he worked at his easel outside the cabin. Two paintings were completed. One would sell to the Governor's Palace in Santa Fe, New Mexico, within weeks after the Jameses departed Arizona. Another, a self-portrait, would eventually be reproduced on the jacket cover of his autobiography. Often, James showed Alice the Russell reproductions he always carried with him and would explain to her what he was trying to do, and with a typical nod of his head when he was impressed, he explained to her the excellence he found in Russell's work.

Although their mail was infrequently delivered, each batch contained illustrating assignments from *Sunset*. Enos Mills, the naturalist writer, had submitted a series of articles to the magazine which *Sunset* wanted James to illustrate. The articles and the drawings were later published in book form.

The encouraging assignments from *Sunset*, however, did not diminish for Alice a basic unhappiness living at the line camp. She had adapted herself to the isolation, and even sensed some of the beauty which James himself saw in the lonely quiet. But she still felt lonely. James seemed to be aloof to her, except when he wanted to talk. Otherwise, he was at his art or in deep, silent thought. To the ways that a woman likes attention and compliments, James was oblivious. Alice cried numerous times when alone in the cabin, or when she took walks out into the desert by herself.

In the evenings, however, James was more sociable. He talked his log cabin talk, a place for him and Alice, or he would reminisce about his past life. Alice encouraged him to talk as it seemed to draw him out of his melancholy and awakened in her a sense that he did need her.

After three months the stock of food had dwindled. James began to wonder if his employer had forgotten them. A few days later the stores were practically exhausted. James turned indignant at the apparent neglect. Alice did not try to console him, and admitted later she hoped his anger would motivate him to want to leave the camp.

When the next day passed and still no supplies were delivered, James declared, "Well, the hell with him." The following morning they packed their bags and walked to the neighbor that had driven them to the line camp in order to hop a ride to Kingman.

CHAPTER SIX

IN KINGMAN, James collected his back pay at the ranch's headquarters. Without any ideas as to what he and Alice were to do next, he took her to a small Mexican restaurant where they sat and talked about their next move. Alice was apprehensive about their meager savings and proposed that they return to Reno and stay with her parents. Mother would be happy to have them, she added, and James could find a part-time job and still have time for his art.

James listened, but had no intentions of returning to Reno. As to Alice's offer that they stay at the home of her parents, "that isn't in this boy's deck of cards as long as I'm dealing," he told her, particularly since her father only mildly approved of their marriage.

James wanted to go to Santa Fe where there was an art colony with western painters, and since the area was good ranching country, he felt assured of a job. After explaining his desire, he said to her, "Saddle up for Santa Fe!"

Alice thought he meant to buy two horses and ride all the way to New Mexico, and she began to express doubt of his proposal. "That would take days and days," she said.

"Your thinktank must be emptying out," James joked. "New Mexico is only a couple of days east."

Alice stared with a hint of annoyance at James. "I went to school, Bill," she said sharply. "I know where New Mexico is and to go there by horseback will take days and days!"

James rolled back in his chair and laughed. "Poor little city girl," he teased, "just knows only that book English."

He explained to Alice that his remark to saddle up meant to travel—and not necessarily by horseback.

They boarded the train that afternoon for Santa Fe.

An intrinsic light and landscape had attracted artists to a small colony in Santa Fe. Even today, it is a haven for artists. To James, Santa Fe was the West for which he had always felt a stirring affection; where the sky belonged only to God, and no symbols of man's abilities poked through it.

"Whenever I get around country like this," he said to Alice, "I feel as little as an ant. The bigger the country, the littler I feel, and the happier I am."

Alice was learning with sharp perception that the land determines the nature of some men. For James, the open country—the desert, the mountains—exhilarated his blood and cleared his mind of self-doubts and inhibitions. He was eager to paint. These were good omens for the dreams and hopes he had for himself and Alice. Unlike Sausalito, Santa Fe's cultural and social atmosphere were horses and cowboys, ranches, and pleasing country. Life there was indolently comfortable for mind and body.

A turn of luck greeted Alice and James when they came to Santa Fe in 1921. A studio apartment in the former governor's mansion had been vacated by an artist only hours before their arrival. It offered a beautiful, deep view to the west, far across the desert and into the hills. Sunset became a time for James and Alice to sit outside and watch the painted evening skies. Alice remembers that at no other time did James express so much inspiration, ambition and utter peace with himself. Not even their dwindling cash could upset him. For Alice, too, the months there were idyllic. James was in a rare mood, sharing his thoughts, affectionate, and attentive.

While other artists painted landscapes or the Spanish element of Santa Fe, James sketched and painted cowboys, their horses, and his renditions of the cow country. He made some minor sales to visiting tourists and local ranchers. One day, an unassuming gentleman offered James two hundred dollars for a painting, one of those painted at the Arizona line camp. Later, James learned the gentleman was the governor of New Mexico. It had happened quickly, spurring Alice and James to celebrate that evening. The sale excited James to a pitch of restlessness, as Alice recalls, but he was wise enough, apparently, to comment that there were bound to be "a lot of ups and downs."

It wasn't much later in the year when the down trend brought them to another serious conference on their immediate future. Their finances were meager, and the few sales James had made with his art weren't adequate to sustain them.

Seemingly, fate was again weaving a close pattern in James's life. If Maynard Dixon had been James's first important acquaintance and his advice to quit art school the first significant counsel he received, then the entry of the Springer brothers into James's life proved to be the second but more influential.

The Springer family had pioneered the northern New Mexico Territory, and the family line still persists in that part of the country around Cimarron and Springer. Frank Springer, lawyer and paleontologist, was one of the principal contributors in supporting the art museum in Santa Fe. Two sons, Wallace and Edward, followed art and ranching respectively. It was Wallace who, in his constant ramblings in the art colony, became attracted to the ranch and horse scenes James displayed. Because of similar interests in ranching and art, a friendship blossomed immediately and Wallace frequently visited James and Alice for long evening talks.

When James realized that he would have to obtain work, he approached Wallace and asked if there was a possibility for a job on his brother's ranch. Wallace replied that he was going to the ranch shortly and for James to come along. Something, Wallace assured James, would be found for him to do.

A few days later, James and Wallace drove to the CS ranch in Cimarron. Wallace explained privately to his brother, Ed, "This boy knows his riggin', but he's on his uppers, and I want to help him out." Wallace also related the tale of James having been hurt by a horse sometime back and asked that Ed give James something easy to do. Ed replied that he would.

Ed Springer had already sent the bulk of his riders up to a mountain camp 9500 feet high in the Cimarron range. He decided to assign James as general caretaker around the camp with the understanding that James could work at his art. The latter was a point Wallace had suggested because he did not want James to neglect his work.

James held his head low when Ed outlined the proposal. Ed studied his expressions and detected that what he had said wasn't sitting comfortably with James. Finally, after some prompting by Ed, James admitted he wanted to ride with the boys—no broncs—but to help with the cow work. Ed acceded to James's wish, more as a favor to Wallace than because of any particular faith in James's ability as a cowhand, of which Ed knew nothing.

With the job secured, James requested a few days to take care of his affairs in Santa Fe. Ed told him to report back when he was ready.

Late that same evening, when James returned to Santa Fe, he told Alice of the job and that it would be best if she returned to Reno for a while. Alice did not want to go, but James insisted that he could not take her to a cow camp. She asked to stay in Santa Fe and James countered that the added expense would keep them broke. She said she would get a job. James cut off that thought without any refining of his language. Finally, Alice consented, and at the railroad depot the next day they separated for the first time.

When James reported back to the CS ranch, acting straw boss John Brewer cut James a gentle string of horses and they rode to the mountain camp. It wasn't long afterwards that James proved his worth as a cowhand. He wasn't sorting wits with rough horses, but on round-up he was roping, branding, and vaccinating with obvious experience. As Ed Springer remembers, James mixed easily with other cowhands. Topping that, James drew pictures for them, pen and ink sketches mostly, that soon were numerous enough to appear as sheets of wallpaper on the bunkhouse walls. James drew his sketches effortlessly, says Springer, and one could conclude that James knew the twists of a bucking horse as only one who had ridden them could know.

About the middle of summer, around July, Ed rode into camp with two companions, Jack Narin, who had a house nearby on the Urracca ranch, and Burton Twichell, dean of students at Yale University. The trio were on their annual hunting trip in the mountains.

In the days that followed James made a considerable impression on Ed and his friends. They had first wondered who the artist was, and during the evenings they sat with absorbed interest as James became a storyteller with a passel of range and horse stories. He told his stories much as he was to write them, in the cowboy jargon, emotionally, convincingly, and interestingly. And if a story lent itself to illustrating, James would sketch the particular twisting actions of a bronc as he talked. He never spoke about his past except as it related to a job at a ranch "up north" or to chasing mustangs in Nevada. To Ed and Jack, James was a cowboy different from the common mixture. To Burton Twichell, experienced in evaluating talents and potentialities of students at Yale, James had more to offer than being a cowboy the rest of his life. A few times, Burton singled out James for short talks with him and inquired as to what James intended to do with his talent. James said he wanted to be an artist and to paint the West as it really was.

One evening, in Ed's tent, Burton and Jack were commenting about James when Burton said, "Ed, I have a scholarship at the university that just fits Bill. It's for artists who aren't qualified to enter by the usual scholarship requirements. You think Bill would be interested?"

Ed summoned James the next morning and told him what Burton had suggested. James was interested, even excited about the prospects. Later, when Burton outlined details of the scholarship, James began to demur. The scholarship covered only the university fees and James admitted he had no savings to carry him through. He thanked the three men for their interest and left the tent.

The next day while the trio was riding to Jack's home, Ed told Burton to reserve that scholarship for Bill and that he (Ed) and Jack would stake Bill for any expenses while learning.

When James rode down from the camp to the ranch on a mail run, Ed called him aside and told him that Burton would reserve the scholarship, and that he and Jack would stake James's expenses. "We feel," said Ed, "that you're a good investment, and if you pan out, you can pay us back."

James accepted the offer eagerly. Afterwards, he wired Alice he was coming to Reno with some good news.

CHAPTER SEVEN

ALICE WAS THERE to meet him when James arrived in Reno at the Southern Pacific train station. He greeted her with fresh and anxious enthusiasm and related the events which led to the meeting of Burton Twichell and said he would be going to Yale to study art.

Alice wanted to know if he intended to take her with him. He told her he couldn't, that their limited funds made the idea impossible. Alice realized that money was an obstacle, but testily confronted him on his casual attitude to their separations.

James, never quite tolerant when facing emotional confrontations, became irritated and impatient. Alice also demanded to know why he believed Yale could be any more helpful to him after his letdown in art school in San Francisco, or why he was taking lightly Maynard Dixon's advice about art school.

James explained that he would be studying under some of

the most talented instructors in the country, and that Burton knew New York magazine editors and would provide introductions. He saw the move as an opportunity, his good fortune, and would not pass it off. If matters brightened, as he hoped, he would send for her.

Alice finally acceded, realizing she could never change his thinking whenever he was totally confident of his own actions.

They stayed with Alice's parents where James enjoyed a reunion with Fred and Elmer and their girlfriends, Dolly and Betty. Betty, Elmer boasted, was a bronc rider who could stick with the nastiest bronc.

James remained only two days before departing for New Haven, Connecticut. While having dinner with Alice's parents on the evening before leaving, he told them that never having had a family of his own, it gave him a mighty fine feeling to be part of this one. Even Alice's father was touched by the sentiment. Afterwards, he displayed his first warming overture to James. They sat together and talked about art and what James hoped to accomplish with his talent in the future.

At Yale, James enrolled in art and English A, a prerequisite course for any entering student. The old traditions at Yale were an interesting side of life James had never seen. His first few letters to Alice were rambling expositions about new sights and expectations.

A week after his arrival, however, the Yale tradition began to press in on him, and immediately his letters to Alice indicated dark clouds rather than the hopeful bright days he had anticipated. His emotions, he felt, were shackled. He was lonely, depressed, and art school was art school, West Coast or East Coast. But most of all, besides Alice, he missed the desert, the hills, and the stock.

This was one of the intense emotions of Will James. It provides a key vital to an understanding of what has been

called the *James enigma*. When he was depressed, he invariably would want to ride into the desert. Whatever it was that
stirred him, he felt humble, content, and secure where nature
abounded. In the coming years when the Jameses and the
Conradts moved to James's Montana ranch, Alice and Dolly
frequently sensed this drama in him and often watched him
walking alone in the foothills that surrounded his ranch. At
other times, he would sit on a rock or the corral fence and roll
cigarette after cigarette and lose the thoughts of whatever
was depressing him by letting his eyes rest on the trees and
mountains and stock grazing peacefully nearby.

His moodiness was always directly followed by a self-
imposed exile on the landscape, or a longing for it. For Alice,
a feeling of inadequacy came upon her when James turned
moody, solemn, and private. But this was only one of several
enigmas that would perplex her. All would be rivals which
Alice could never completely comprehend and against which
she couldn't compete.

Yet, even though life at Yale mostly depressed James, he
had his good moments while in Connecticut. Burton took a
paternal interest in his progress and invited him to eat at his
home many times. At the university James roomed with another art student named Webb Overlander. He didn't particularly care for James because "James threw the bull too
much." Nonetheless, they did spend time together, and
Overlander recalls his acquaintance by a few incidents.

"I remember one time we were in a cellar on campus doing
some weekend work for the school when James came upon
some Remington prints that were stacked away. He sat there
for hours studying them and smoking his Bull Durham cigar-
ettes one after another. I finally finished my work and waited
for him. But after a while I got tired of waiting and left him
there. I don't think he even heard me say I was going."

James also began to drink again when he was at Yale. As a

cowboy he earned his fair share of credits drying up bottles. But since marrying Alice, he had rarely drunk.

Overlander recalls that James "put on a couple of dillies."

"One time, he came into the dorm drunk as hell. He was sort of half-crying while muttering something under his breath. All I could make out was something about a murder in Canada; Alberta, I believe he said. But he had fooled them and burned the log cabin jail and escaped."

Overlander thought it was just another of James's tall tales and never gave it a second thought. James would slip again with that remark to Alice at their Montana ranch while he was drunk. The significance of the story will be discussed further on.

After two weeks of school, he wrote Alice that he was quitting. Upset by his actions and knowing he was lonely, Alice borrowed money from her father and went to New Haven. In the meantime, James explained to Burton that he could no longer tolerate art school. He wanted to do what he felt he had to do, and art school was artificial, frustrating, and a hobble to him. Moreover, he wanted a studio of his own where he could work. James was completely confident that he could produce good and salable material as he had done for *Sunset* magazine. But he needed better markets.

Burton was sympathetic to James's thoughts about art school and sensed in him an anxiety and impatience with anything that restricted him from expressing what he wanted to portray on paper and canvas. Frequently, James showed Burton the historical errors of other illustrators in the New York-published "western" magazines. A critic himself, Burton challenged the interpretations of James's own sketches. James was always prepared to defend his art. To a letter of 1922 (after James returned to Nevada) in which Burton had criticized some sketches of James's cowboys, the artist answered:

The criticism you handed me was good and I appreciate it by the fact that you wish me to keep improving—but I can say (not to stick up for my work, but only for the trueness of what I put out) that in my drawings, even the cowboys may look long waisted. What makes him look that way is the way he wears his clothes. His waist line is below the hips. That's where his breeches and chap belt rests and what makes him look longer that way. Other folks wear theirs way up above the hips, but they don't have the freedom of movement the cowboy's got to have. . . . As for aquiline faces, sharp hook noses and such, you're right there. What I've done is put all the cowboys I've seen and known along with myself in the same pot and all boiled down I got one character what covers over seventy-five percent of the range riders. . . . All of us makes the same mistake if you call it such. You can tell a Russell, Remington, Leigh, Wyeth or Dixon cowboy far as you can see 'em . . . they all got one character same as I got mine—it's just how they see the cowboy—it's why some are truer than others.

Burton, although he may have had some doubts about James's style, believed him to have the talent to make the top grade. And since James had said to him, "To win big, one has to play big stakes" (meaning the New York magazines), Burton made arrangements to take James to New York to meet some of the top magazine editors.

Meanwhile, Alice's arrival in New Haven was a gratifying surprise to James, although she had not been quite certain what would be his reaction. Officially, James had been dropped from the university but was presently a house guest of the Twichells. They now also welcomed Alice.

A few days later Mrs. Twichell, observing that Alice had few clothes, least of all a warm coat, took Alice shopping with her and insisted on buying Alice a winter coat with a fur collar. While Alice was delighted when she showed James her new coat, James was visibly embarrassed. Seemingly, he swallowed his pride, realizing how few things Alice owned, and told her how nice it looked on her.

About a week later Burton took James with him to New York. James selected his best drawings to show Charles Dana Gibson, editor of the old *Life* magazine which at the time used primarily illustrations instead of photographs. Gibson did not hesitate to heap verbal praise upon a glowing James and told him that his drawings had life in them. James commented he would rather have them in *Life*. They talked mostly about James's background and his natural propensity to art. Gibson expressed awe that James did not work from models. The cowboy explained what he was attempting to do—draw true visual representations of life in the West—as opposed to the mythical presentations that were more popular with magazines in the eastern part of the country. Gibson was impressed with the young man and later confided to Burton that he could well understand why art school was too narrow for what James was trying to accomplish.

Gibson offered some suggestions to James and told him to assemble a set of his drawings as he had for *Sunset*, and to call again.

After leaving Gibson's office, James was bent upon letting out a war whoop. Burton snuffed the urge by telling him they were in the wrong place for such exuberant antics.

A week later, with financial assistance from Burton, James and Alice moved to New York. They found an apartment on West 86th Street. In his first letter to Burton, written from New York, James wrote:

"Yes sir it all looks mighty good, and to think that if you had not made that little trip to the Cimarron country and been the kind of man you are, I might be setting traps for a living this winter or else hazing a herd on the winter range."

James worked diligently on a set of sketches for *Life* magazine and visited with Gibson again to see if these ideas were developing satisfactorily. Gibson restated his enthusiasm, and a few days later James submitted his portfolio. Gibson told him to come back after the next weekly editorial board meeting.

James patiently waited out the week. To Alice, he kidded about how they would spend "all that money *Life* would pay." But when James returned to the *Life* office, all he received was Gibson's regrets. The editorial board, Gibson explained, liked the sketches and saw much merit in them. But it wasn't quite what *Life*'s editorial board felt suitable for its magazine.

Gibson expressed his personal disappointment. He encouraged James to go on, emphasizing that one magazine was not the whole publishing world.

Life's rejection had sapped James of the bulk of his hopes. What annoyed and confused him was that he offered authentic sketches, and he could not understand why eastern magazines contented themselves with half-truths in the illustrations they did accept.

James wrote Burton that what he would have to do with *Life* was to "just educate them to it . . . to sketch something to their liking at first and then afterwards to submit my own feelings in the sketches. That was how I had done it with *Sunset*." He also bet Burton two hundred dollars that within a year he would sell to *Life*. James would lose that bet, but only because within a year another magazine would be taking all he could offer.

In the meantime, however, he and Alice were again struggling against their dwindling savings. James made a few sales to *Sunset*, but there seemed little expectation that he would derive enough earnings from the magazine to allow him to stay in New York for further probing of the eastern magazine market. Burton had offered James a loan but James declined, since he had already discussed with Burton a loan in order to build a studio in Nevada.

James, while grateful to Burton for his help and advice, believed that his entire New York venture was a discouraging setback. Sending him further into depression was the beginning realization that his oil painting techniques could not stretch to the greatness he admired in Russell. The harder James worked in oils, the more he realized Russell's exceptional talent. It wasn't easy for James to admit to himself that pen and pencil techniques could not easily be duplicated in the grander medium. He said to Alice that it looked as if he had reached his plateau in oils. And he knew that level wasn't good enough.

He needed only slight encouragement from Alice and they were on their way back to Nevada.

CHAPTER EIGHT

RELUCTANTLY, James followed Alice's advice to move into her parents' house. He bemoaned the feeling that he was imposing. Staying at the Conradts after all the expectancy of New York was a sure indication that he had failed. "I feel like a licked dog coming here," he told her.

But there was fun, too, coming back to Reno. Frequently James and Alice along with Fred and Elmer and their companions went riding, using horses from nearby ranches. There were all-day trips to some of the ghost towns in western Nevada, or jaunts to small rodeos at stock ranching areas such as Fallon, Smith Valley, or Lovelock.

In the early summer of 1922, *Sunset* magazine informed James it had illustrating assignments for him. James went to San Francisco where he stayed for two weeks as Maynard Dixon's guest.

While James was away, Alice decided to find a place where she and James could live and which would allow her husband more room for his work. Her brother, Paul, heard of a studio apartment for rent west of Reno on the Coughlin ranch located on a hillside with acres of rolling sagebrush. When he took her there, Alice knew this would be a place for them. She wasn't certain what James's reaction would be. Money was still scarce although the *Sunset* assignments and a few commercial art jobs for local businesses had helped. But she felt a studio for James would be an encouragement.

After James returned and Alice showed him their new home with his own studio, he was ecstatic. It would cause a pinch, he admitted, but was worth it all. But they never felt that pinch, as the ranch owner agreed to lower the rent in exchange for James attending to a few daily chores on the ranch.

Fred and Dolly were married that same summer and moved to the Walker Lake country where Fred was hired to manage a ranch. Three months before, Elmer had married his lady bronc rider and they were living in California. The hell-raising days of the one-elevens were now just a memory.

James stayed close to the ranch and his work. Except for Sunday dinner at the Conradt's, he had little interest in going places. But he was restless, not as a fiddlefoot but in his mind. He was resigned to the realization that he would not be an artist as great as Russell; yet, he intensely desired to create some artistic presentation of the western theme.

In early fall, and somewhat suddenly, but with perfect harmony to his sketching, James began to write. Alice had frequently prodded him to write during their marriage. To her, writing seemed the simple and logical thing for him to do since he told stories effortlessly and with a colorful choice of language. Until this time, James had always shunned the idea. Now the thought caught his interest.

In discussing it with her, he was doubtful, however, of an ability to write the way editors would want, meaning with proper English. "Besides," he said, "if *Life*'s editors turned down those sketches, what do you think they'll do to something I write?"

Alice countered James's argument with his bias about unauthentic western stories, saying that his language, at least, would be of the real cowboy. She even suggested he write a story about bucking horses since that was all he ever seemed to talk about.

A week later, James showed Alice an article written in longhand and with a dozen illustrations. He titled the article "Bucking Horses and Bucking Horse Riders." He wrote it just as if he were seated on his haunches with some buckaroos at a cow camp and telling his stories. He told Alice it was "too easy done to be any good."

Nonetheless, James sent the article to *Scribner's Magazine* with all expectations it would be returned to him. For days afterwards, Alice also became apprehensive, not about the article, but what its rejection could do to James. He tried to cover any concern for his first effort, and when Alice would go for the mail, she sensed how he tensed himself in expectation of seeing the envelope he had addressed to himself when he submitted the story. She wished he had not banked his entire hopes on that one story. And there were moments when she wondered if perhaps she should not have encouraged him so persistently to write. Great expectations, she realized, have the lurking shadow of great disappointments. She worried that the return of the article might discourage James from any further writing and possibly dismantle what he had so far built with his art.

For James, doubts grew because he saw in his work no similarity to what was currently being published. He failed to realize that this difference, rather than signifying mediocrity, actually made his story an exceptional piece of regional writing, an emotional narrative with an accumulation of interesting details making a reader feel.

Scribner's Magazine accepted James's first article and paid him three hundred dollars. For two days James could hardly believe that something he had written was to be published by an "eastern outfit" and he constantly re-read the letter of acceptance. His confidence and ambition soared and he immediately set himself to writing other articles in hours-long sessions. Frequently he wrote and sketched until dawn.

In their acceptance letter, the publshers asked James to write a short preface about himself to accompany his article.

The preface James wrote is a defense of the article, an almost bragging notice that he was a real cowboy who lived the cowboy life extensively, as few other writers did.

It was a strange preface since a perceptive reader could sense that the article was written by a cowboy. Even more, the deep sensitivity in the way the story is told also assures the reader that its author must have lived the experiences. James, however, did not realize how well he had told his story. Maybe he was even psychologically over-compensating for his fabricated early life.

"Bucking Horses and Bucking Horse Riders" is a description of western horses and the men that tamed and rode them. It qualifies as one of James's best writings by carrying with it a strong and truthful scent of western life, drawing energy from James's feeling for a people and a culture which had been made by the land and livestock.

This was the inkwell James plunged deeply into after Scribner's accepted his first piece and, in longhand, wrote a series of stories about the manners and mores of the cowboy.

"A Cowpuncher Speaks," a mirroring of the western country the way it had been before social and economic upheavals, conveys a strong feeling of James's sentiment for the open range days and the sad plight of the nesters who settled with hopes of planting a crop. James tells his story through a character named Jim Austin, a ranch owner confronted by nesters. For the nesters, there was never enough water. As James tells, "It was a cow country and should have been left such; but the nesters kept on hoping and working; the little money they'd brought with 'em was gone, and the little homestead was all they had. Some writers would have it that the stockmen hired gunmen to drive the nesters off, but I'm here to say that I've packed many a hunk of beef on the back of my saddle for a certain nester with plenty of family and no grub."

James tells the story of Jim with interjections of his personal observations, as though to set the record straight.

But as James relates, the nesters stayed, the range changed, and "Jim couldn't follow the old trails much more."

Scribner's Magazine readily accepted "A Cowpuncher Speaks," and with more assurance than it had accepted "Bucking Horses and Bucking Horse Riders." As James later learned, the editorial department was doubtful of his first submission because of its unconventional English and clashing grammar. The art department, however, was quite taken with his illustrations, and on their insistence the article was accepted.

Readers' response both to story and illustrations was highly favorable and prompted the magazine to accept readily 'A Cowpuncher Speaks."

The *Saturday Evening Post* purchased "Pinon and the Wild Ones," an excellent account of wild horse trapping. Then *Sunset* informed James they were feeling neglected, so he sold them a three-part article called "Bronc Twisters." With these same stories, James also produced some of his best illustrations.

Success had been sudden, and James's financially barren life changed to one of abundance. He was paying off debts and now had money in his pocket and in the bank. It was an opportune time for him to buy his first car.

He and Alice went to a Reno dealer. After some initial pricing, James decided to purchase a 1920 Pierce Arrow. "That's the one," he told Alice. As she was to learn, James always picked the biggest car to buy.

The salesman asked James if he wanted any instructions in driving the car. James said he did not. Alice had never seen James drive a car, but assumed he knew what he was doing. He found reverse, backed out of the garage like a bronc coming out of a chute, and hit a telephone pole on the other side of the street. He stood up on the car seat and yelled to Alice who was standing stunned in the garage driveway, "I spurred it too hard!" A week later the repaired car was delivered to James at the Coughlin ranch.

Scribner's Magazine bought two more articles, "Cattle Rustlers" and "Cowboys North and South." *Sunset* accepted "Desert Range Riding" and was also now paying him three hundred dollars an article. James suggested to Alice that it would be nice to have that place of their own with a few horses and a studio.

James had looked at a parcel of land between Reno and Carson City at Franktown in Washoe Valley that completely suited him.

Washoe Valley is one of the more beautiful areas in western Nevada. From the steep Sierra mountains, the land glides gently down to level pastures and then to desert growth where it meets and rises gradually to brown tinted hills in the east. On the Sierra side of the valley, thick with pines, James purchased five acres. It afforded a panoramic view of the valley and a clear sight to Washoe Lake on the valley's eastern side.

James desired only a cabin and went to Alice's father for advice on materials and building. To his surprise, Alice's father and two brothers, Bill and Ed, said they would build the cabin for him and Alice.

It was a four-room cabin with a large fireplace in the parlor. An especially large window was installed allowing a broad, clear sight into the valley. On the eastern side of the house, corrals were built for three horses which James had bought. Adjacent to the corrals were built a small barn and tack room. Above the house, where the pines were thick, James built his studio: a log sanctuary with a stone foundation, just large enough for his writing desk and art materials.

He now had his studio, his cabin, and his horses. Those wistful dreams he and Alice frequently talked about were now very much real. And with these roots, he felt content to enjoy the pleasures of his own land and his own home.

Each morning, after breakfast, James went to the corral to feed the horses. While they ate, he sat on the corral railing rolling his cigarette and thinking. He enjoyed being alone, especially when in deep thought, and sometimes would sit quietly and motionless for over an hour. Many times Alice watched him from the cabin as he chain-smoked, and she often wondered what it was that held him so deep in thought. Then suddenly, he would hop off the railing and head for his studio. James left definite instructions for Alice that he was never to be disturbed while he was in his studio, not even by her. He would come for lunch if he were absolutely hungry. At first, Alice had lunch prepared for him, but later resigned herself to prepare his meals only if he appeared.

In the following months, James's accelerating career was tantamount to a fairy tale success story. He wrote nothing that did not find a willing publisher. *Scribner's* took "The Longhorns" and "Making of a Cowboy," while the *Post* bought "Once a Cowboy." Calendar companies approached him for his illustrating services, and *Redbook* asked for a story.

Western pulp magazines, some of which had previously rejected James's art, now asked him to illustrate for them. Between writings, he worked with renewed interest on oil painting.

Although James would not think of the title for some years yet, he was already the "lone cowboy," much to Alice's dismay. Not infrequently, he would arise before she did and not return from his studio until early next morning. She drifted into lonely wanderings around the ranch or went horseback riding on the trails behind the cabin. For a while, she blamed herself for his inattention, but soon realized that he was just not the ideal husband. He withdrew too excessively within himself and his work.

Yet, Alice was intelligent and empathic enough to realize that she had married a talented man and some exceptions to conventional behavior were to be expected of him. She felt that in time he would accept his writing as a job with only so many hours to be devoted to it. She waited anxiously for his adjustment to success.

Alice had wanted a child soon after their marriage. James, reasonably, felt that they could not afford the expense. With him now making steady sales and to all indications, a success, she revived the idea. Again, James expressed disfavor. Alice, deeply hurt, vowed she would never ask him again, and she was more convinced than ever that James should not have married. He exhibited too much selfishness, not with material things, as he often bought her presents, but within himself, and for his work. With his first articles, he frequently sought Alice's advice about sentence structure, spelling, or other story ideas. Now he never consulted her, and she never knew what he had written until it appeared in print. Once, after reading one of his articles, Alice offered what she believed to be a constructive criticism. James became resentful and down-graded her suggestions, since the editor, he said, thought it good enough to be accepted.

Fred and Dolly frequently visited on weekends. Not often would James interrupt an entire writing day for them. He usually went to his cabin for at least a morning of work. In the afternoons and early evenings they socialized and took horseback rides.

One weekend, James mentioned to Fred a foreman's job that was open on the Elsman property next to James's, and how nice it would be if Fred and Dolly lived close by. They thought so too.

James introduced Fred to Mr. Elsman and, within an hour, Fred accepted the position. The foursome spent considerable time together, and the few years they were to live near each other would nurture deep attachments.

By spring of 1924, James had a considerable number of manuscripts in the *Scribner's* office. The publishers informed him that his articles, including those in *Sunset* as well as recent submissions, would be published in book form.

Cowboys North and South appeared in October 1924. James had good reason to be proud of the book for the critics themselves uttered the praise that James wanted to hear. The *Times* of London suggested that the sketches of the artist, Will James, "had nothing to fear from comparison with the work of Frederick Remington or any other artist of the plains."[16]

The *New York Times* book reviewer was also complimentary, but with an ironic observation:

"Let the skeptic reader be assured at the start that the book makes excellent reading in spite of its handicap of truth. The author evidently combines keen, logical insight with a rich sense of romance. While confining himself to facts, the facts he brings forward are by no means dry."[17]

Cowboys North and South provides a literary pleasure for its reader, an unfiltered look at the last horsemen of the range in the last decade in the age of horse culture. In "Bucking Horses and Bucking Horse Riders," included in the book, James shows eloquently what is real to him. To the eastern reader especially, a bucking horse is a bucking horse. When James wrote of broncs, however, he had his reader experience the convulsive twists, grunts, and tricks of the bucking horse and the pounding a rider takes while aboard.

In the article "Cowboys North and South," the lead story in the book, James reveals a range country knowledge that has all but been forgotten. He describes a time when western riders' customs, equipment, hat styles, horses, and round-up procedures indicated their regional origins: the Spanish-influenced cow country of the Far West, the buckaroo country of the Northwest, and the Texas way. James lived the cowboy life during the tail end of those regional distinctions, and before Hollywood, circuit rodeos, and mass saddle production eclipsed local artisans and made "cowboy" the singular name of all riders who now saddle and dress very much alike.

"Winter Months in a Cow Camp," is a pleasant reflection of isolation and cattle chores in snowbound cow country, and the whoop-it-up joy experienced with the coming of spring.

The book was a critical and financial success for the publishing house, and Scribner's immediately saw in Will James the sort of writer whose name and style could sell more books. Maxwell Perkins, Scribner's astute editor (also consultant to Ernest Hemingway, Scott Fitzgerald, Thomas Wolfe, Marjorie Rawlings, etc.), wrote James a suggestion for developing his naturalistic writing style.[18]

December 5, 1924

Dear Mr. James:

I suppose you have seen enough reviews of "Cowboys North and South" to know with what enthusiasm the critics and literary observers have received it, and as much on account of the text as the pictures. I have enclosed a review that has just come from Struthers Burt; but, the comments of the ordinary unliterary citizen, who is really the important critic in the end, would probably interest you more, and, if so, those I heard would please you much. As for the sale, it goes well and promises to go better.

Anyway, the outcome of the publications has already been such, it seems to us, as to give you any assurance you may have wanted of marked success in book writing; I hardly think you could have had any doubts at all upon the matter of illustrating. I am, therefore, writing to suggest that you consider following this book with another written in the same manner but different in design, a continuous narrative with as much or as little plot as you thought best, which would bring into the compass of a single story the adventures and incidents characteristic of a young cowboy's career, related in his own words. Really, the book I have in mind—for unsatisfactory as comparisons are, one can never altogether avoid them—is ''Huckleberry Finn.'' There was very little plot to it, you probably remember. Its great interest was simply in the incidents and scenes of the trip on a raft down the Mississippi, told in the language of a boy. Of course, ''Huckleberry Finn'' is primarily a boy's book and it would be better if what you would do were not altogether that, but the great thing is that any such consecutive narrative would give your unquestionable talent for graphic human writing a chance beyond that which this book gave. And we suspect that it would show an equal skill in making types and characters realizable as individuals. Won't you consider this? We should then have a book of novel size, to sell as a novel, and would be quite justified in having great expectations for it. We, of course, see it also as illustrated with your own pictures. I have talked to Mr. Chapin about this and he is in hearty accord with the plan.

CHAPTER NINE

JAMES SETTLED into a less rigorous writing schedule after the release of *Cowboys North and South*. For the moment, at least, after having soared high since acceptance by *Scribner's Magazine*, he had expressed much of what he felt about the West and the cowboy.

In that same rush, Alice believed that she had learned more about the man she married. Through his writing, mostly autobiographical, she sensed the loner in him from which sprung the emotional side of Will James that made him respond to the West as he did. It was best presented to her in one of her favorite passages from his writings:

> As I'm setting upon this little knoll taking a last look at the country where I'd put in so many hard rides, a little old coyote ambles up the side of the hill, sees me and stops, starts to run some more, then somehow feels I'm harmless and stops again. I see him limping and notice a trap kept one of his paws. He, too, has been

crowded a heap, and somehow I have more admiration
for him than I used to. I'd like to let him know we're not
enemies no more. . . .

The next few years of marriage became easier for her than
the previous four. She now accepted, without prolonged bewilderment, his often inexplicable mannerisms, his periods
of sullenness and crabbiness, and realized a man like himself
was not pliable to the pattern of a conventional husband. He
had refused to have children, and although Alice did feel
hurt, she could excuse James, since he never really had
known what family life was like.

Still, life with Will James had been fast paced. What were
dreams only yesterday, when they talked of log cabins, a few
horses, and a studio, were now a reality. And James's writings and art were bringing in considerable funds and much
recognition. They travelled extensively to rodeos, stock fairs,
and autograph parties where he was frequently introduced as
the West's best cowboy artist and a true son of the "Golden
West."

They had a small group of mutual friends, particularly
Fred and Dolly, although James seemed to know anyone that
wore a hat and boots. Often, too, Alice's family visited on
weekends.

For Alice, the pattern of life in the Washoe Valley was
becoming predictable and comfortable.

Even while this pattern was settling, James was starting to
hint about a move. Nevada, he claimed, was beginning to
crowd him and he wanted to go where there weren't any
fences and where cattle were still worked on the open range.
When Alice asked where, James answered, "My birth state,
Montana."

She didn't like the idea. It meant an upheaval, leaving her
family and generally upsetting everything that had now come

to be a pleasant way of life. James detected that Alice did not share a particle of his enthusiasm to move to new country. Finally, he said it was mostly a thought . . . "to throw a ketch rope on some other time."

His output of articles continued. Scribner's was receiving most of his stories since they planned to publish another book of his articles. For *Sunset*, James fulfilled a contract for two articles to be submitted by the year's end of 1924. He sold them "First Money" and "When Wages are Low."

Neither article is outstanding. Possibly James was rushing his stories at this time, since as he hinted to Alice with his usual noncommittal grin, he was working on a lengthy horse story about his "Ole Smoky horse," the story idea Maxwell Perkins had suggested in his letter.

In his small studio in the pines James worked in long bursts of seclusion detached from Alice, Fred, Dolly, and the outside world. Still, when he did emerge from his isolation, he was happy, filled with gusto, and smiling. Instead of the long writing sessions having fatigued him, he was only the more enthusiastic to get back to work. To neither Alice, Fred, nor Dolly had he ever talked much about what he was currently writing, but from sense of pride, he discussed the horse story he was now writing.

James labored on Smoky and its illustrations for almost a year. He interrupted the novel for additional articles for *Scribner's Magazine* and one relating to his work in the movies for the *Southwest Review*.

In December 1925 Scribner's published the second volume of James's articles under the title *The Drifting Cowboy*. It was critically treated to the same compliments that greeted his first book. Again, James's illustrations were most favorably noted: "as vigorously alive as a young bronc on a frosty morning," commented the *Bookman*.[19] Lawrence Stallings in *Outlook* wrote: "Will James has a distinct literary style. He has that and more, and the Scribner's have had the good judgment not to translate the book into English."[20]

In April of 1926, and prior to book publication, *Scribner's Magazine* published the first of four lengthy installments of "Smoky, the One Man Horse." The cover of the magazine heralded the equine hero with a watercolor done by James, featuring Smoky and his one master, Clint.

Smoky appeared in book form in September 1926 with forty-three full-page halftone illustrations. It drew the best reviews James was ever to read about his books. William Hornday called it "one of the truly great horse stories in our language!" The *New York Times*, in a simple but high-reaching compliment, said, "Will James has done the 'Black Beauty' of the cow country."[21]

Smoky went into a second printing in September, another in October, two more in November, and five more in December, and it has never been out of print since.

The epic horse story is James's best fiction, and its illustrations are his best single group of drawings. James missed nothing in describing the life of the range horse. The first two chapters, where James describes Smoky as a wild range colt, are a clear evidence of his keen observation of equine behavior and his love for horses. *Smoky* reverberates with realism. Even more important, the narrative expresses the feeling of love for a horse that moves a reader's emotions. It is the essence of James's talents at their best. The book is also the best indicator of a way of life he did know—the cow country just before and after the First World War.

Smoky was a real horse. James was riding a large blue roan stallion that he called Smoky when he rode into the eastern Nevada country around 1913. Riding with him was a saddle pal named Fred Allen, a tough, heavy-drinking cowboy who rode a horse similar to Smoky. Both horses were the only ones of their kind in that part of the country, and it appeared they had probably been raised at the same ranch and sired by the same stallion.

Only James was capable of riding Smoky. He had won bets from other cowboys who vowed they could ride the horse. James encouraged them to try by claiming that Smoky was a one-man horse. Apparently no one could ride Smoky unless they understood his bucking pattern. Smoky would buck with James too, and without provocation, but James knew the routine Smoky followed and was able to stay aboard.

In James's years of storytelling in reference to Smoky, inconsistencies crop up. In *Lone Cowboy* James wrote, "instead of the horse [Smoky] being a company horse he was my own."[22] Years later, he wrote in *Horses I've Known*, "Smoky wasn't my own horse. I only broke him for the outfit I was riding for at the time."[23]

And going further about the horse, which also demonstrates James's usual inclination to be evasive, he plays a nonsensical game with his readers in telling where Smoky was born:

"Mentioning the outfit where Smoky was foaled and raised, I will only say that at one time, when I was riding for it, it had cow camps and headquarters spreading in most every western state from Mexico to Canada. . . .

"For an identifying clue, that widespread outfit about lost all their cattle, many, many thousands in one year, and went to raising horses."[24]

Most likely James was hinting to the enormous Miller-Lux Company. Most interesting, however, is his attitude. It may appear insignificant, but basically it typifies James when he spoke about himself. His statements were vague and often teasingly generalized.

Critical and public reception to *Smoky* lifted James to a measure of recognition he never expected. He attended autograph parties in Reno, San Francisco, Denver, and New York where he also conferred with Scribners on future books.

Royalties from *Smoky* were pleasing too, and perked again James's hope of moving to Montana. But now his dream enlarged to a cow ranch of his own in a country that had not been torn by fences.

He slipped the "ketch rope" off the thought he had expressed to Alice some months before and told her specifically of land on an Indian reservation near Billings. It suggested isolation to Alice, but a ranch of their own also carried pleasant thoughts and a dream of the wide open spaces for which James pined. She agreed to move, as did Fred, whom James wanted as foreman of the ranch. Except for Elmer, who died suddenly only three weeks before, the old pact of the one-elevens to share a ranch was becoming a reality.

Selecting Fred to manage the ranch, however, was not merely to satisfy that early promise. Fred had considerable experience managing a cow and calf operation, and since James was admittedly "damn lazy" other than when he had to write and draw, he needed someone dependable. Fred was never to falter, even when he was to be torn between loyalty to James and concern for his sister, Alice.

Selling his property in the Washoe Valley was unexpectedly easy for James. There was a neighbor who complained to James on several occasions that his horses were causing a fly problem.

After James and Alice had decided to move to Montana the neighbor visited again to lodge a complaint. James met the gentleman on the front porch and rolled a cigarette as the neighbor instructed James on the proper disposal of waste to curtail breeding areas for insects. When he finished, James quietly told his neighbor that he would not have to worry any longer about garbage, bugs and horse manure. "I'll be movin' shortly," said James. "Expect to sell out to a pig farmer."

The visitor sat speechless for a disturbing moment.

"Pig farmer?" he ascertained.

"Pig farmer," drawled James.

"Has he bought yet?"

"Nope," replied James.

"I'll buy."

For years after, James delighted in telling the story of how he sold his Nevada property.

Montana was a fulfillment of James's notion of the great outdoors and the great West. Essentially it had been tamed, but still the breath of mountain men and trappers lingered in the mountain country, and Billings still had the aura of the active cattle center and cowpuncher town it had been. James had been enchanted with Montana when he rode that country as a cowboy. He liked best the Crow Indian Reservation lands in southeast Montana, near Pryor and forty-five miles south of Billings. It was a land very much alone to itself, unfenced and about the size of the state of New Jersey. About fifteen hundred Crow Indians lived scattered across the reservation. Some had made modest success on their land as ranchers while others were content to lease their land to the white man.

James purchased dead-Indian land—land subject to sale because no heirs had made claim. His initial purchase was four thousand acres. Over the years, with additional leases, the ranch was increased to eight thousand acres. He selected for the home ranch a valley almost completely surrounded by red sandstone cliffs in the foothills of the Pryor Mountains.

While James and Fred searched about the area, designating buildings and corral locations, James expounded on the local history. He told Fred how thousands of buffalo once roamed the area and where, still, bands of wild horses were less than two hours' horseback ride away. On the other side of the reservation was Custer Battlefield where remnants of the 7th

Calvary were outwitted by the Sioux and Cheyenne. It was an area James often frequented. He liked to sit on the high cliffs where Major Reno and his men had retreated after the Indians had chased them across the Little Big Horn River.

After selecting building sites and completing business transactions in Billings, James returned to Nevada, leaving Fred to start erecting the buildings with hired labor. When James arrived at Washoe Valley, Alice had completed packing and arranging for the furniture shipment to Billings. Dolly, meanwhile, had moved in with her family in Reno and was to wait there until Fred had built their home on the ranch.

The evening before James and Alice were to leave for Billings, James complained of an ache in his abdominal region. By morning he was experiencing intense pain and Alice drove him to a Reno hospital where he was operated on for acute appendicitis. Impatiently, James remained in the hospital while Alice vacated their Washoe Valley home and moved in with her parents in Reno.

About April 1927 James was released from the hospital and, with Alice, went directly to Billings. They rented a hotel room but expected to be there only about a week before moving into the ranch house. James went to the ranch each day and soon was discouraged at the slow progress in building. Two weeks later it was apparent that he and Alice could not stay at the hotel without considerable expense. As Fred and his crew were living in surplus army tents, James purchased one for himself and Alice and pitched it close to where their home was being built.

James made an effort to write, but it was difficult for him to concentrate with all the construction work noises. Each morning, after a talk with Fred, James took his writing pad and climbed to one of the bluffs overlooking the building activity.

One morning Alice suggested to James that he should assist Fred to speed completion of their house so James could get to his full schedule of writing. James answered, "I got to make money to keep us going."

Probably no one but James realized how true that was. The land, its buildings and corrals, labor, and the stock he was ready to purchase had put him deeply in debt. To climb out required a regular flow of writing. Although James had so far held to a respect in his writings about life in the West, his debts and obligations, and his future plans for the ranch, forced him to bend that respect. He was writing his articles quickly now, and was playing up the Wild West motif. Alice recalls that an editor or two had suggested to James that he add drama. In fact it was even necessary, they insisted, since popular markets are not entirely oriented to pure truth. James made a protest to one editor, but was told that his magazine was not interested in James's revolutionary crusade for the true West. James was in no position to argue the matter. He continued writing a flood of articles, some of which he gave the tall yarn.

While still in Nevada, he had started a series of articles for *Scribner's Magazine* titled, "All In A Day's Riding," which would continue periodically into the early part of 1930. The *Saturday Evening Post* published "On Circle," "Remuda," and "Round-Up Wagon" and had a stock of articles that would cover their pages until 1928. While the *Post* and *Scribner's* became the more prolific publishers of James's writing, *Youths' Companion* was happy to receive some contributions, and *Ladies' Home Journal* assigned him illustrating work for stories with a western theme.

By August, the ranch was finished and alive with stock. Fred went to Reno and returned with Dolly in time to celebrate with James and Alice a telegram from Scribner's notifying James that *Smoky* had won the prestigious Newbery

Award presented by the American Library Association for outstanding literature for children. Sales of the book jumped and Scribner's prepared to issue *Smoky* in its Illustrated Classic Editions for which James was to add color illustrations.

Smoky did not win the award without protest from some quarters, as James was later told. That the story itself was good was not denied, but objections were lodged against the cowboy vernacular.

The point was well-taken. Words such as *figgered* and *sashayed*, the bad grammar, the spelling of *creature* as "crethure," and the slang expressions caused the resentment toward the book. Time has proven the objections to be invalid in view of the many fine qualities that *Smoky* possesses. Well-written myths of the West were worse to some critics than truths written in a vernacular that, in spite of bad grammar, had as their essence an honest story told effectively.

Moreover, there is a certain and skillful portrayal of the horse, Smoky, which James avoids muddling into an overly sentimental and slobbering tale of an unfortunate horse. Nor is there the humanizing of the emotions of the horse, the bane of so many horse stories.

If he had written no other book, *Smoky* would have assured him a significant place in the literature of the West.

CHAPTER TEN

JAMES NAMED his ranch the Rocking R. It became the embodiment of what he hoped would restore the idea and vision of the old West. He wasn't overly concerned with newer agricultural techniques and the changing economics of ranching. "Rope 'em and brand 'em like the old-timers," he instructed Fred and ranch crew during round-up.

Publicly, James also confirmed that he wanted to "keep alive what was passing in the west,"[25] and collected on the ranch artifacts that satisfied his desires.

One of his first aesthetic whims was a small herd of Long-horns he had shipped to his ranch from Oklahoma. To friends and guests James enjoyed expounding on the history of the Longhorn and the great trail drives; how those rangy, all-legs-and-horns cattle fed the nation after the Civil War with cheap beef until railroads, fences, and fancy English cattle changed it all. He would compare the Longhorn with the old-time cowman, both of which he said were "tough and independent." The newer cattle breeds, he added, like the new cowboys, were pasture fattened.[26]

Occasionally, James's indulgences annoyed Fred since these were usually charged against the commercial cattle operation which Fred was attempting to make self-sufficient. Nonetheless, he understood James's motivations and told Dolly, "If that's the way Bill wants it, I guess I can understand his mood."

Still, James, probably after discussion with Fred, did import from Texas a few head of the large Charolais breed of cattle for cross-breeding experiments with Herefords to develop a hardier cattle for the Montana winters.

Alice also became chagrined with James's excessive attempts to keep a frontier-like tradition alive on the Rocking R. Most annoying, and humiliating, was James's refusal to allow an inside bathroom.

An outhouse, Alice told him, was just out of date in these modern times. James persisted and, over the years, delighted in observing the amazed dismay of his guests, especially those from the East, when inquiring for the facilities. He also pointed out to them the creek where they could bathe.

Alice did win a concession by having a room at the Grand Hotel in Billings permanently reserved in James's name for guests willing to make the drive from the ranch, and for Alice and Dolly who made the trip frequently during the week to bathe properly.

(About a year after moving to the ranch, Alice threw some rags soaked with an inflammable fluid down the outhouse hole. James went to the outhouse with his inevitable cigarette, which he tossed into the hole. Alice heard a large *boom* and rushed out of the house. James came staggering out, his face blackened with ash and visibly scared. He looked at Alice and said, "My God, the damn thing blew up." Alice never revealed that she may have been the cause, although James surmised that *someone* had thrown *something* down there.)

Nor did James permit the one road to the ranch to be paved. Its washboard pattern became one of the jokes in Billings which informally named it "James's kidney rocker." But he didn't mind such drollery. He said in an interview for a Billings newspaper that "because my part of the country has poor roads is why I like it."[27]

The only fences were the pole corrals for holding and the stock pole fences around the main houses to keep stock away. Otherwise, it was open range between Rocking R and whatever adjoining ranches had erected their own boundary fences.

Out of the foothills, deer, antelope, elk, and even cougars roamed through the ranch with James's guardianship as he permitted no shooting. He acquired a pet deer along with pet rabbits, dogs and cats, which he and Alice were especially fond of. These also were allowed to run free over the ranch.

His most satisfying luxury was horses.

"We had more horses than we ever needed," Dolly recalls. "But horses were the one animal Bill wanted around the place. It made no difference whether we needed them or not. If Bill liked a certain horse, he bought him, even the drafty work horses which Bill had a special sympathy for.

"Many times Bill would wander to the corrals and spend time with the draft horses. One day when I had finished milking the cow and was leading her back to the pasture, I heard Bill under a lean-to speaking to the team of Percheron work horses we had. He said: 'Old-timers, they're taking away all that's good in the West. You too.'"

Dolly smiled when she heard James talking to the horses. In looking back, she remembers James at his kindest and most gentle when he was with the animals, especially with horses.

For Alice, also, her first year on the ranch was memorable and exciting. She was experiencing a closeness and sharing with her husband she had not previously known. On a new land which was their own, and a ranch house which the two of them had designed, they shared discussions about the furnishings, hung photographs and James's favorite drawings, and mutually created an expansive western motif.

Together, or with Fred and Dolly on weekends, and frequently with guests, riding was a constant recreation. They explored every foot of their rolling ranchlands, right into the Pryor Hills. Often there was overnight camping, sometimes by themselves but frequently with ranch visitors. Guests went away with their own memorable introductions to western hospitality on the Will James spread.

And always, Alice recalls, there were invitations to ride in rodeo parades in Billings, Helena, or Missoula. In all, in her first year and the few that followed, she found herself a close and intimate part of an experience that was the growing aura of Will James.

She no longer was as distressed by his self-imposed periods of isolation when he was working, or his periodic and unexplainable moodiness when he sulked along with a reluctance to talk. But there were times when his remoteness was so prolonged that she hoped for visitors to break his spell and bring him back to his geniality, gaiety, and western waggishness.

Not infrequently, James detected Alice's vexation caused by his aloofness and would surprise her with a gift of a new riding habit, saddle, or a horse. Like all his surprises, pleasant or frightening, James would spring them when they were least expected.

At a time of innocence, but a seed time of stress, Will James sits at the knee of his father, Jean Dufault. James was nine years old and already displaying the talent for drawing cowboys and horses that would lead him to the American West. His brother Auguste is seated next to his mother. Standing are James's sisters Eugènie (left) and Helene. (Courtesy of Auguste Dufault)

In his first year in western Canada James was all buckaroo, but more in appearance than ability. Taken at a cow camp on Sage Creek in Alberta, close to the northeastern Montana border in 1907. (Courtesy of Alice James Ross)

"30 YEARS AFTER"

James, in this tattered sketch made while he was working on a Nevada ranch about 1914, displays his eternal romanticism and his sadness over the passing of the old West. It was to haunt him all his life. (Courtesy of Gertrude Gottschalk)

This sketch was done around 1916 while James was neither cowboy nor artist, but an inmate of the Nevada State Prison in Carson City. It is one of four found stored in prison records and is now housed in the Special Collections Department of the University of Nevada, Reno, library.

The 111s (one-elevens): Elmer Freel, Will James, and Fred Conradt in Reno, 1919. (Courtesy of Dolly Conradt)

James sold his first art in 1919, receiving fifty dollars for two drawings used on poster cards and a rodeo program. (From the author's collection)

Joking time. Alice and James at a line camp in Arizona, late in 1920. The oil James is working on is a self-portrait, eventually used on the dust jacket of his autobiography, *Lone Cowboy*. (Courtesy of Alice James Ross)

James and Alice, at their cabin home in Washoe Valley between Carson City and Reno around 1923. In this idyllic setting, James wrote his most lasting and popular book, *Smoky*. (Courtesy of Dolly Conradt)

"What the Cowboy wants is a head-fighting, limber-back cross between greased lightning and where it hits." From "Bucking Horses and Bucking Horse Rider," James's first article, sold to *Scribner's Magazine*. (From *Cowboys North and South*, 1)

"The black was jerked off his feet, rolled plum over, and he lit head first on the other side." (From *Smoky*, 2)

"With life, action and humor, which almost tears out of every page," said the *Literary Review*, November 28, 1925. (From *Smoky*, 2)

"I puts my bed on one, my saddle on the other, and away I go."
(From *Drifting Cowboy*, 3)

Alice and James about 1928, a year after moving to their Montana ranch. (Courtesy of Alice James Ross)

Dolly, Clint, and Fred Conradt around 1933. (Courtesy of Alice James Ross)

The making of the "lone cowboy." James, depicting himself, when under the tutelage of his fantasy guardian, the French wilderness trapper Bopy. (From *Lone Cowboy*, 6)

James and friends on a Sunday outing at the Rocking R Ranch in Montana. (Courtesy of Alice James Ross)

"Then my rope sails out and snares him." (From *Sun Up*, 4)

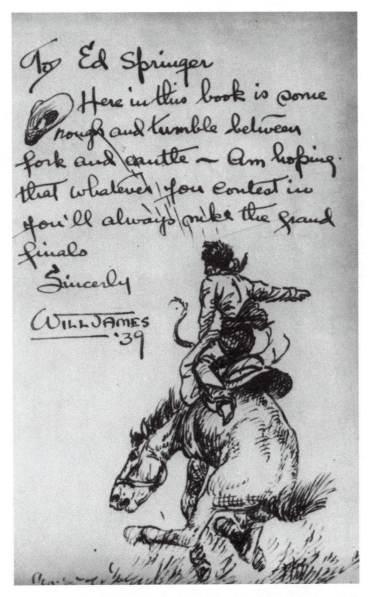

Fly-leaf inscription in *Flint Spears*, sent to James's benefactor Ed Springer in New Mexico. It was Springer who, said James, "backed his beliefs with a heap more than words." (Courtesy of Ed Springer)

One of the many moods of horses which James excelled in expressing. (From *Scorpion, A Good Bad Horse,* 5)

Near the end of their first year on the Rocking R after James had been sullen for over a week, he quietly went to Billings and returned an hour later without any explanation. Next morning at breakfast, he told Alice, "Your folks will be here in a couple of hours. Better get to Billings to meet 'em."

James had wired train fare to Alice's parents together with an invitation to stay at the ranch as long as they wished.

During this first visit by Alice's parents, her father confided to her that he had certainly been wrong about James. He said he was happy that James had done well for himself and Alice and apologized for his mulish attitude against her marrying him.

Cow Country, James's third volume of stories and recollections, appeared in October, 1927. Again, the critics praised his work. One of the collected stories entitled "Complete," is almost biographical of his own nostalgic and restless nature.

The story's hero is "Dude" Douglas. Similar to James, he is a cowboy who has tired of drifting. James introduces "Dude" as he is riding night guard around a bedded herd . . .

There's many things come to a cowboy's mind at such times: the quiet of the night, the dark shadow of the big herd, and the steady swing of the pony's gait are all, it seems like, in cahoots to bring out what might be buried the deepest in a man's think tank. And it was as that cowboy was riding along and sort of keeping his eyes on the edge of the herd that particular night, that the dark shadows of cattle and horns begin to sort of evaporate, and as what came to his mind took shape, there came visions like a timbered hillside, then a creek with quakers and cottonwoods along it, and by them cottonwoods a rambling log house and corrals—his own log house and his own corrals.

James weaves a tale of a gentle but growing hunger as "Dude" yearns to settle down on a place of his own. "Dude"

soon exchanges bucking horse work for the more gentle oc-
cupation of riding into his pastures and estimating the weight
of his steers. But the rambling fever still persists and ham-
mers at "Dude" to follow the seasons throughout the cow
country. Even as he follows this urge, he feels homesick for
his spread. It is only when he finds the right gal, marries her,
and returns with her to his ranch that his life and happiness
are complete.

The story of "Dude" is one of James's better short stories.
It has the feel of the earth in the days not so long ago when
earth, a spread of one's own, was what most western men
felt a need for.

It was a story which reflected James's ideal for himself, but
which his own reality would not allow.

Alice could not point to any particular time when the in-
solvable problems came between them, but they began that
first year at the Rocking R. Slowly, beginning amorphously,
they took shape over the years, generating turbulence as they
grew. James's drinking, his strange disappearances without
telling her of his departure or destination, and his inability or
refusal to account for large sums of money brought on arguments and recrimination which settled nothing. All they did
was develop in Alice a realization that her husband was becoming more and more enigmatic.

There were incidents during ranch parties for movie stars,
publishers, or other dignitaries, incidents when James drank
excessively, when he would tell stories about his early life
which were inconsistent with what he had previously related
to Alice. At first, she questioned him about what he had said
(usually a story about his days with the French trapper,
Bopy), but James became evasive and countered that Alice
must have heard him incorrectly.

Contrary to what Alice believed, that James's heavy drinking started after his success, it was a habit noted long before he was married. His records at the Nevada State Prison indicate this, as do recollections of those who knew him during his riding days in Nevada. With marriage, however, and detached from free-wheeling cowboys, and with his compulsion toward art and writing, he had rarely indulged in a single drink. But after success had lost its polish, he became easy prey to drinking under encouraging conditions. At ranch parties, his drinking was frequently an embarrassment to Alice. More than once at rodeos he would leave Alice in the grandstand and head for the chutes to carouse with the cowboy contestants, and not return. Sometimes he had a note delivered to her saying he had "gone with the boys for a spell." James might return by himself, but increasingly a group of cowboys would carry him back drunk.

Alice, Dolly, and Fred never ceased to be awed over how James ever completed his work. But his work was his strongest devotion and one that drink did not override at the time. But when he finished a book and announced to Alice, Fred, and Dolly that he had "a new one packed and on its way," habitually he started a three- or four-day drunk. It became a twilight existence in which he seemed unaware of what he said or did.

Dolly recalls these episodes as her saddest memories while living at the Rocking R.

"It was frightening and pitiful. He often scared Alice. Once he took a pistol and poked it into Alice's ribs and cocked the hammer. He wasn't angry. He just thought it was funny. A few days later Fred told him what he did, and that the gun was loaded. Bill went to Alice and cried as he apologized. He just never seemed to know what he was doing when he drank."

When in such a state James was uninhibited. The turn of a thought in his mind was quickly enacted. Once in New York, he led the rodeo parade. Suddenly, he reined his horse off the street, rode into a prominent hotel, and shot at the lobby lights. Texas, Hollywood, and Montana also would be branded with James's wild cowboy capers.

Once, after James acted in an embarrassing way at a party, a mutual friend approached Alice and suggested that she was to expect a certain amount of capricious behavior from him. He was a creative artist, after all, and didn't he usually get to work afterwards and produce a good book?

Alice tried to believe this interpretation at first, but soon saw its fallacy. What tormented her was James's moody dispositions that did not result in creativity, but instead in nasty insults to her, to guests, and sometimes to Fred and Dolly who were least deserving of James's abuse.

There were times when Alice screamed at James to tell her what was bothering him, wanting to know if it were her or something that she did or was not doing. James, if he did say anything, offered an excuse too trivial to be the cause of his vagaries. Alice knew he was lying. James, aware that she sensed his insincerity, might take the car and drive away. Two or three days later he would return and without excuse or apology go to his studio.

When his drinking and emotional irritability subsided, he was as most people knew him: kind, gentle, a charming story teller, tolerant, and fun to be with. He was, as if repenting, overly gentle and generous with Alice, and this behavior would cast a renewed glimmer of hope for her that their marriage would last.

CHAPTER ELEVEN

IN HIS FIRST winter on the Rocking R, James started a new novel he titled *Sand* and worked on the set of oils for the classic edition of *Smoky*. He also decided that he would not winter at the ranch again.

He told Alice that the coldness hampered his work. More likely the feeling of being hemmed in, literally snowbound, made him restless. He enjoyed excitement and recognition. Winters ceased altogether the riding parties, the picnics, the rodeos and parades, the summer dances and singing.

What he planned for himself and Alice was to spend summers on the ranch and winters in San Francisco, Santa Barbara or Los Angeles. He promised himself that he would write two books a year with that living arrangement and, for the most part, fulfilled that obligation.

Sand was almost finished the following summer when James and Alice went by train to New York for a conference with Scribner's. The publishing house also scheduled an itinerary throughout the metropolitan area for James to lecture and autograph books.

An apartment was rented on Madison Avenue. The first few days, James conferred with the Scribner's editor, Maxwell Perkins, and also with Whitney Darrow, a vice president who managed James's business interests with the firm. Darrow agreed to his author's request for a sizable advance against royalties to offset operating expenses at the ranch.

Perkins suggested to James some rewriting on *Sand* and gave full approval of the sketches for the new edition of *Smoky*.

Sand, James expected, would be another writing plateau for him, something he had not attempted. It was a romantic novel, in the *genre* of Zane Grey, about a dude that becomes a cowboy, tames a wild stallion and wins for himself the horse and the heroine.

There was additional business also at the *Ladies' Home Journal* office. James had recently completed illustrating for the magazine a Hal Borland story, "Haven," and now they wanted James to do drawings for a Mary Roberts Rinehart story, "Dude West." And the *Saturday Evening Post*, which had also recently accepted James's "The Big Hat," conferred with him for new work.

Alice had hopes that she and James would travel through upstate New York. He agreed to the idea; but at the time, neither was expecting the overwhelming response to James's talks and book-autographing parties. Fans swarmed to the sessions to see this exotic individual from the West; to hear him talk in his picturesque language and curious grammar. As always, James wore western clothes and boots. To the kids he was like the second coming to the East of another Buffalo Bill. James reveled in the attention heaped upon him at Macy's bookstores or New York's horse society groups. Particularly amazing and touching to James were the kids who delighted in the man who wrote *Smoky*. They asked him to tell stories and draw pictures. James always obliged them in the simple and plain cowboy talk they wanted to hear. "Someday," he told Alice, "I'm gonna write a story just for kids who want to come west and can't. I know how they feel."

Evenings were no less demanding. Social affairs were frequently given in his honor by magazine publishers, and literary and library associations.

One afternoon James telephoned Alice to tell her that he was bringing Charles Scribner to the apartment for dinner. Alice told him not to be too early as she would have to go out and shop. James instructed her not to get fancy and that franks, beans, and some biscuits was what he wanted to have served.

Alice refused even to consider such fare for one of the East Coast's most esteemed and urbane publishers. James, in the firm way which Alice knew never to question, repeated what she was to prepare.

As Alice remembers, Scribner enjoyed his evening, listening attentively to James expound about the West, his ranch, and the food he was raised on. Hot cakes, he told Scribner, were also a favorite of his, and artichokes when he was on the West Coast.

When Scribner prepared to leave he thanked James for a delightful evening and he complimented Alice on her franks, beans, and biscuits. It was, he told her, "refreshing in its simplicity."

In October, the rodeo at Madison Square Garden opened with much western fanfare. James was to star and introduce each event, and to present trophies to winning cowboys. An exhibition of his drawings decorated the lobby as did copies of his books which eager readers purchased to have him personally autograph.

While the rodeo was in town, Alice hardly saw James, and neither did Scribner's who frequently called her asking for the rewrite chapters for *Sand*. Alice told Scribner's, as she told others who inquired for James, that he was with the cowboys—wherever they were at the moment.

On the train coming to New York, James casually outlined to Alice a new horse story he hoped to start while in New York. Now, after a social whirl and overnight disappearances by James with the rodeo cowboys, Alice reminded him of his new story idea. He replied that the book would have to wait until he got back to the ranch as he hadn't the time. Alice countered that there would be time if he would stop going to every party to which he was invited and stop carousing with cowboys. James didn't agree. It would be rude, he said, to act stand-offish.

By April, 1929, James turned fickle again and grew tired of New York. *Sand* was finished except for additional sketches. He told Alice that they were getting back to the ranch where he could get something done.

Within a week after arriving at the ranch, James mailed the *Sand* sketches to New York and turned immediately to completing the oil paintings for the classical edition of *Smoky* due to be published in 1929. The paintings were also scheduled for exhibit in Montana, Texas, New York, and Los Angeles.

Sand appeared in May and was assaulted by the critics. In general, the book was considered far below the standard of James's best work. Van der Water in the New York *Post* was the most fault-finding:

"Will James's drawing are as good as usual, but his text is deplorable. A novel, after all, demands something more than draftsmanship and a perversity in spelling. Further, Mr. James's smug belief that all virtue is sequestered between the Missouri and the Rockies, irritates us a trifle."[28]

Sand was insulting to the easterner as Van der Water protested, showing him as a city bumpkin fumbling in a westerner's world. He wins his spurs at the story's end, but only after proving himself worthy of a westerner's respect.

Bad reviews rarely disconcerted James. What would raise his hackles, however, was criticism from editors or reviewers that his written language sounded phony, or needed some "Englishizing." No one, he stated to Alice, was to change his writing. That was the way he talked and the way he wrote, and editors could take it or leave it.

A critic once said of James that his language was not in the cowboy vernacular. James angrily replied that his talk had been picked up and mixed from the different localities of the cow country. The language of the cowboy, as he noted, "is just as different as the style of rigs and ways of working." James liked the cowboy tongue, and possibly he did over-use it for commercial emphasis.

While critics, as said, hardly upset James when they showed only lukewarm attention to his books, he nonetheless was critical of them. There was a strutting cockiness in James's attitude about his books. He felt because they were written by a real westerner, this in itself made them unique. Critics did realize this, and weren't reticent about heaping praise on his books when it was due. What James failed to realize was that his writing was losing a particular sheen by the time *Sand* and recent articles came to the public. He would do better writing after *Sand*, although a decline is nevertheless noticeable.

For the first time, in late 1929, Alice wrote her mother about her differences with James and implied that unless he changed, she would leave him. Her mother wired Alice immediately that James probably needed her more than ever. Alice wasn't convinced. She had told James she would leave him unless he stopped drinking. James wrote to her mother, pleading with her to convince Alice not to leave. This pattern became commonplace, with Alice finally being persuaded by her mother to stay with James.

At other times James wrote to his mother-in-law telling her that she was the mother he never had and that she understood him better than Alice. Grievances between James and Alice were painfully felt by Alice's mother.

It is curious that neither Alice nor James ever asked for a divorce. In spite of simmering resentments and arguments, neither suggested that solution. George Snell, James's attorney, told James that unless he did stop drinking, Alice would leave him. Snell pointedly told James that he was in sympathy with Alice. James admitted to Snell that he drank too much, and that he still loved Alice. Yet, he would never say those words to her.

In November 1929 James arranged to leave for New York to see his publisher. Alice wanted to go along with him, hoping to keep James to moderation in his drinking. He told her plainly that it wasn't necessary for her to come with him. His business would not take long, and since they planned to stay the rest of the winter in San Francisco, it would be best if she went to the West Coast to locate an apartment. Alice agreed, and James promised that he would return within three weeks. This winter, he said, he wanted definitely to write that horse story which he had been mulling through his mind for nearly a year.

They said goodbye at the Billings train station with Alice eliciting another promise from James that he would not drink excessively and would hurry back.

Shortly after, Alice left the Rocking R and stayed in Reno for a visit with her family and then went on to San Francisco. She found an apartment and wired the address to James at Scribner's. James answered that he would be finished with his conferences soon. Shortly after he sent a letter indicating his immediate departure from New York. Alice presumed James was on his way to California.

Nearly two weeks later with no sight of or word from James, Alice called Whitney Darrow. He told her that Bill had left New York ten days before, presumably bound for California. Alice called the hotel where James had stayed. It informed her James had checked out over a week before and left no forwarding address. Alice wired Fred in Montana, telephoned her mother in Reno. Neither had seen James. Alice became frantic, fearing the worst, especially if James had been drinking.

Meanwhile, Whitney had done some checking on his own. He learned that James had sent a telegram to a dentist friend in San Antonio advising of his arrival. It was Christmas Eve when Whitney telephoned Alice. She told Whitney she had no knowledge of Bill having friends in Texas. Whitney admitted James had been drinking heavily. He felt it would be best if she went to Texas. "If he's still drinking," he told her, "it could be a whopper, and he'll need you."

Alice telephoned for train reservations and was relieved to learn she could start later that evening, making train connections at Los Angeles for Texas. Her mind during the entire trip was filled with premonitions that something had happened or was going to happen to James.

When she arrived in San Antonio, Alice immediately telephoned the dentist named by Whitney but received no answer. After an hour of unsuccessful calling, she registered at a hotel. Knowing that James would not stay at anyone's home if he could stay at a dude ranch, she started calling local dude ranches.

At the sixth ranch called, a woman proprietor admitted James was there. She wanted to see Alice first, however, and would come to her hotel.

Upon arrival, she told Alice that James was in a terrible state. She did not like his drunken behavior around the ranch, but refrained from calling the police since the papers might hurt his reputation. She also told Alice that James said he was separated from his wife, and that he had lost a lot of money in the market crash. Alice was bewildered, wondering if they were speaking of the same man. The woman said there was no mistake. She also suggested that it might be best if Alice did not come to the ranch, as she feared more unpleasantness by James if surprised by Alice. The proprietress preferred that Alice give her a note for James and wait to see what would happen.

James came to her hotel room about three hours later, fairly sober but bedraggled. Alice did not question him as to why he had come to Texas, or why he had made those remarks to the ranch woman.

"I think you better go home to your mother," he began. "You can get along without me."

Alice knew he didn't actually want her to go. Usually, after he had sobered from a humiliating drunk, he felt punitive measures necessary against himself. For Alice to leave him seemed to befit his recent actions. They talked for hours. James again and again suggested that Alice leave him. She knew, too, she couldn't leave him. He was forlorn, wretched and to leave him would be abandonment. Besides, she reminded him, they had planned to do his life story together, and she wouldn't leave until that book was written. She also reminded him that he had promised to dedicate it to her.

The writing of James's life story had also been suggested by Whitney. Through Alice, he learned about James's boyhood with Bopy and of James foraging on his own over the West when he was about fourteen. The matchless saga of his life seemed a natural for the printed word, and Whitney had on a few occasions urged its writing. It had, he felt, enough marvelous adventure to top *Smoky*.

James agreed with Alice to write his life story. When it was finished, he told her, she was to leave him.

She rented two typewriters, as James wasn't too steady for writing legible longhand. Alice wrote to her mother and to Fred explaining what she and James were going to do. She called Whitney also, who immediately became excited about the book's prospects. He instructed Alice to start sending in the chapters as they were finished. Type would be set and chapter proofs returned immediately.

Four months of typing by Alice revealed to her for the first time the complete story of James's life. She saw him differently now, excusing many of his irritating ways because the life he had led was so different from that of most men. She felt sorry for him, and wondered if a man who had always been so alone, so self-reliant, should ever have married. He had often told her that he couldn't help himself for the way he acted at times. Maybe, Alice thought, he was being truthful. He couldn't help himself.

James interrupted writing *Lone Cowboy* to do a review of Charlie Russell's *Good Medicine* for the New York *Herald Tribune*. The book was a collection of letters by the artist and were assembled by his wife, Nancy. James also wrote an introduction for *French Heels to Spurs*, by Loraine Fielding, a story of an easterner going to a dude ranch in the West.

James wrote about six hours a day. In the evenings he worked on the drawings to accompany the story while Alice typed final copy. Maxwell Perkins called repeatedly telling how excited he was about the book. "It could only happen in the West," he told Alice.

By May 1930, *Lone Cowboy* was finished and the Jameses returned to their Montana ranch. James's bitter thoughts that

Alice should leave after the book was finished seemed to have been forgotten. The only recent argument was the time when James at first refused to mention in the book that he had married. He thought it detracted from the idea of his being a "lone cowboy." Alice insisted that his marriage gave the book a proper and normal ending.

Scribner's, who had hailed Will James as *the* writer on rodeos, round-ups, ranch life, cowboys, horses, stampedes and the whole West, now gave the public *Lone Cowboy, My Life Story*, by Will James. Reviews were enthusiastic and the book scored rapid sales. The *Review of Reviews* stated, "If there is anywhere a cowboy saga, we have it here."[29] The Book-of-the-Month Club made it its August 1930 selection, and there was talk that the book might be made into a motion picture. At year's end, James's autobiograpy ranked fifth as a best-seller in the nonfiction list of 1930 and boosted him to the apex of his career.[30] He was now of legendary proportions, a magical name in one of the most emotionally stirring sagas of the American West, a saga which had caught the public's fancy. Only he knew, however, that with *Lone Cowboy*, his career and his integrity were balanced on a precarious suppression of his true credentials. He became a man marooned with a stifled self, an unrelenting inner terror which, after the world-wide attention to *Lone Cowboy*, increasingly fragmented the man and his personality.

CHAPTER TWELVE

LONE COWBOY is the story of a man alone in the wonderland of the American West. To the imagination already perked up to the idea of a glorified West, *Lone Cowboy* sharpens and refines, excites and stirs the emotions. But not in sweeping generalities. Instead, it focuses on one man living an adventure, Will James, and crystallizes a reader's identification and empathy.

Lone Cowboy begins near the turn of the century with the pathos of a little boy, Will James, orphaned in the great Montana range country. James says his parents were moving toilsomely by wagon from Texas to Canada when in June 1892, James was born "close to the sod," near the Judith Basin.

"If I could have seen far enough," he writes, "I could have glimpsed ponies through the flap of the tent on my first day while listening to the bellowing of cattle and the ringing of my dad's spurs."

James writes that he does not remember his mother, a Californian of Spanish and Irish-Scotch descent, as she died shortly after James was born. Her maiden name was Rodriguez, which James claims as the origin of his middle name, Roderick.

James's father, born and raised in West Texas and a cattle drover during the eighties, was killed by a maddened steer while working on a ranch when James was about four years old, according to *Lone Cowboy*.

To a friend of James's father, a French trapper named Jean Beaupre, James was entrusted.

Together they traveled the wilderness trails north into the Peace River country of Canada and along the Mackenzie, setting trap lines and living at isolated camps. James describes himself as practically a child of nature, with nature teaching her own the lure and lore of her ways. He learned that when the geese flew north in the spring he and Bopy, as he called his guardian, would abandon their snowshoes. They would take to saddle and pack horses, ride south over mountain passes and through valleys into the United States and into the cow country for which James felt a strong affinity. And when the geese heralded their southward course, the boy sensed that he and Bopy must ride north, exchange their saddles for snowshoes, and again settle to a winter of trap laying.

Education?

Catalogues, old newspapers, and magazines picked up at the ranches or found in abandoned cabins afforded James the only hints of other ways of life. For as James tells it, Bopy was a wanted man and shunned civilization. Still, the wilderness patriarch informally taught the boy to read French. And, with greater exactness, James was taught the ways of living off the land and on the land—covering a fire with grass and causing a smoke smudge to keep away the mosquitoes because, Bopy told him, "if you kill one the others get peeved and pick it out on you."

When Bopy took to the course of his trap lines, James had to rustle and amuse himself in a line shack as he awaited Bopy's return. He had a horse to ride, but within geographical limits sternly ordered by Bopy. While still very young, James felt the urge to draw, and used charcoal from the fire to express with natural aptitude the forms of wild animals. But his favorite theme was cowboys and their horses. The urge to draw was unremitting in those lonely days and Bopy, recognizing the boy's pleasure, gave him pencils and pads of paper as New Year's gifts.

Often alone, restless and inquisitive, James describes the unusual events which filled the spacious vacuum. He tells the story of the time he adopted two wolves, *Gros* and *Otay*, as pets. He remembers shooting his first bear with Bopy's muzzle loader when he was about ten. Then there was the year of agony while his stomach healed from burns received from drinking a can of lye he mistook for a can of milk.

These were the wilds and the dangers of his life as a youthful nimrod. And yet he never fails to tell about the beauty of the country, or the drifting back and forth with the seasons over the great western landscape when it was still primeval and still challenging.

When James was about fourteen, he writes, personal tragedy searched him out again. Early one spring morning Bopy did not return from fetching water at a river camp. James searched for him, but found only Bopy's water bucket that the current was battering against a river bank. James reports feeling a premonition, but all day he searched the country and called for Bopy while his emotions tingled with fear that he had been abandoned. That night he slept fitfully, his first time alone, and cried when he awoke.

For the next few days he rode his horse up and down the river, still calling and searching, all the while fighting a gnawing sensation that Bopy had drowned. Finally, he accepted his feeling and knew he would never see Bopy again.

James struck camp, packed the horses, and, continuing the pattern of living Bopy had taught him, rode south to the cow country. He was completely independent now, and alone, but seemingly never lonely.

James's *Lone Cowboy* tells stories of life in scattered cow camps. He was still too young to be an experienced buckaroo, and his life as a rider began by helping the cook wash dishes, riding night herd, listening to the old cowboys tell stories, riding his first bucking horse, chasing mustangs, and competing in small rodeos.

But he never stayed anywhere very long. He was a tramp cowboy with a packhorse and an unrelenting urge to drift, to see new country, and to find new experiences.

James rode from the cow country of the North to the cow country of the South—from Canada to Mexico.

In *Lone Cowboy*, the uniquely emotional account of James's early orphaning and adoption by Bopy is a mirage, an essentially innocent lie that began with the lightness and fascination of a single snowflake. It made Will James preeminently attractive, but after *Lone Cowboy* it became a weighty avalanche comprised of guilt and fear of exposure.

The "facts" are fiction; and yet, beyond the margin of the lie itself, there is recognition that the love of the West and the courage of young Will James in *Lone Cowboy* were no less than the love and courage he possessed when he was known as Ernest Dufault who, at the age of fifteen, left his home in eastern Canada to venture as a cowboy in the West. At that time Ernest was not unlike many boys in the East whose dormant spirit of adventure had been stirred and made restless by tales of westerners in pulp magazines. He liked the romance of the cowboys, the awe of wide open spaces. But above all, a love for the horse anchored Ernest to persistent longing to someday go West and become a cowboy.

James was born Joseph-Ernest-Nephtali Dufault on June 6, 1892, at St. Nazaire de Acton, in the province of Quebec, of French parentage. His father, Jean, was a merchant and his mother, Josephine, a deeply religious and devoted mother. Both parents were born in Quebec province: Jean Dufault at St. Nazaire de Acton in 1852, and his wife, thirty miles away at St. Ours, in 1863. Shortly after James's birth, the family moved to Montreal where James grew up.

Ernest was the second child born. An older brother was named Phillipe, and another, Auguste, was seven years younger than Ernest. Three sisters completed the family: Anna, who later became the Reverend Sister Cajetan, Eugenia, and Helene. Of all the children, Ernest was the most sensitive and intent. He loved to draw and the use of a pencil or crayon came to him as naturally as life gave him the involuntary act of breathing. By the time he was five, his parents were astonished to see Ernest lie on the kitchen floor and on a piece of wrapping paper draw pictures of cats, dogs, and horses; childish scribblings to be sure, but with attention to proportion and detail. Ernest's mother was certain that God had blessed her family with a child genius.

Before he was ten, however, an accident almost took his life. He had come into the kitchen and, seeing on the kitchen table a bottle of white liquid which he thought to be milk, drank a few swallows. The bottle held liquid lye. Ernest's screams brought his mother rushing into the kitchen. She quickly forced him to drink milk to ease the burning pains and sent Phillipe for the family doctor. When he arrived, the doctor induced Ernest to vomit. Later, he told Ernest's mother that her quick action had saved Ernest. But for a year he was a sickly boy. It pained him to eat, and while his stomach healed from the burns, he stayed on a liquid diet. He was often remote and withdrawn with an absorbing interest in pulp magazines.

Ernest's father owned the Hotel Union, a small boarding place where Ernest could collect abandoned pulp magazines with their action stories and illustrations. He couldn't read or understand English, but would cut out the illustrations to take home and copy.

With his brothers and sisters, Ernest went to a Catholic school. As each of the boys completed his primary schooling, he turned to work to help support the family. Ernest worked as a bellboy and kitchen helper at some of the local hotels, and often he earned extra money by sketching, with soap, pictures of horses and trapping scenes on the plate glass mirrors behind bars of saloons and hotels.

Trappers were abundant in Canada at the turn of the century and their gathering spots were favorite haunts for Ernest. There he heard the trappers tell tales of the white wilderness to the north and of the animals that inhabited it. While the trappers told their stories Ernest would frequently sketch their descriptions. It is from this association that James wove the story of his life with Bopy in *Lone Cowboy*.

While trappers and their tales aroused Ernest and sparked his desire to travel to the western country, his love of the horse became the focal point of all he dreamed to do in his life.

He often told Auguste he wanted to ride horses in the wide-open spaces—a dream which was certainly the one spell that clearly dominated his entire life. His dreams to go West never faltered. He often proclaimed to his father that he wanted someday to be a cowboy, but this was accepted as youthful infatuation that would pass.

When he was fifteen he solemnly announced to his mother and father that he was going to the Canadian West. They did not want him to leave. But his father seemed to know that with or without permission, Ernest would go. His mother thought him too sensitive to be alone and on his own. Ironically, it was this same sensitivity to a calling that was his courage and drive. In 1907, with ten dollars from his father and the prayers of his mother, Ernest went West.

As he traveled westward probably on a harvest excursion of the Canadian Pacific Railroad, seeing the country change from small congested communities to the wide expanses of western Canada must have given rare pleasure to those wild longings in his heart.

For about three years he stayed in Saskatchewan and Alberta country along the U.S. border. Presumably, some of the jobs were not unlike what *Lone Cowboy* describes, after Bopy has drowned and Billy (James) is on his own. Nighthawking, helping the cook, cutting wood, and at every chance working horses and livestock are all plausible pursuits for a youngster on his own and willing to learn the cowman trade. Even some of the amusing incidents described in *Lone Cowboy* are probaby those of Ernest when he learns to smoke and takes his first drink, or when one of the riders sees Billy incessantly scratching himself and tells him, "Why, you little son of a seacook . . . you're lousy as a pet coon."

Ernest's first visit home was in 1910. He stayed only briefly and then returned to Alberta. It was probably just before Ernest went home that he had his first encounter with the law.

It has been mentioned that when James was enrolled at Yale he did some loose talking, through liquor, that he had once been on death row in Canada and had escaped by burning a log cabin jail. Again while intoxicated (in the early thirties), he made the same remark to Alice.

In *Lone Cowboy* James relates an incident involving a sheepherder in a saloon fracas that caused James to be confined in a post stockade of the Royal Canadian Mounted Police.[31] The sheepherder became indignant—"on the prod"—and, pulling a razor, cut across James's left ear and down his cheek. James retaliated by shooting the herder. James, in a dazed state, and after receiving medical treatment, returned to his hotel room. Shortly after, the Royal Northwest Mounted Police came and arrested him.

The next morning James was told that the sheepherder had died. For weeks James was confined and then suddenly was released. He went back to the bar where the trouble happened to see the bartender who was on duty the evening James shot the herder. James was informed that the bartender was no longer working because he was in jail for shooting a sheepman.

What had happened, according to James, was that the herder ran out of the bar when James shot him. After James returned to his room, the herder returned to the bar and began to pick on the bartender, who promptly obliged the "scrap" by spinning him with another bullet. The bartender, believing he had killed the man, ran away and James was held. Not until after the police were able to gather the complete story did they release James.

James probably reworked the facts about the sheepherder incident when he wrote the story in *Lone Cowboy*, as he also doctored the facts about his cattle rustling in eastern Nevada. Whether the herder died is unknown. But if James did burn the jail and escape, as he later said while intoxicated, it may have been after the escape that he went home in 1910. He now told his family to address all letters to him as C. W. Jackson and that he was going to cross the border into Montana. Dropping his French-Canadian name and going to Montana, he said, would offer better opportunities for himself. A few months after his departure he changed his name again and informed his family to address him as W. R. James.

About the summer of 1910 James presumably crossed back into Saskatchewan. At Gull Lake, in the southwest corner of that province, he asked for a job from Fred Jackson who was running the round-up wagons for the 76 Cattle Company. Jackson was then in his early twenties and remembers James riding a "fuzz tail of a horse who couldn't throw a wet saddle blanket." James wanted to hire on as a buckaroo. "Somehow," says Jackson, "he just didn't look like a buckaroo. He was awkward looking on a horse. I offered him a job as wrangler, and he took it. He was an awful poor cowboy at the time and no good in my book."

Jackson took a dislike to James because James couldn't measure up to his boasts of being a top hand. James wrangled for two months, left a flock of drawings for some of the riders, and quit at the company headquarters at Crane Lake.

The earliest account of Will James is related by a contemporary of James named John Crouch.[32] Crouch, in his letters, is uncertain if he met James in 1910 or 1911 in the Texas Panhandle country.

James and Crouch became acquainted when James rode into a ranch where Crouch was working. They became fast friends and decided they would ride into Old Mexico for the winter.

"When we got to Monterrey, Old Mexico, we decided that was deep enough in Mexican country. So we camped on a little stream outside town and just wandered around several days. Then we got on with a big cattle outfit . . . gathering cattle off the range for shipment. We worked over a month at that."

After the job, James and Crouch camped on the creek, eventually becoming friendly with a nearby Mexican family. Their Spanish was limited, according to Crouch, but they learned enough words to spend frequent evenings visiting at the Mexican home.

"I have set by a campfire with him many a night. He wasn't a runaway talker in those days. I have seen him sit as much as an hour not saying a thing. He seemed to be thinking. And when he would say something it might pertain to horses or cattle.

"He told me the same words he wrote in one of his books. . . . Said if he had been born one month sooner he would have been a Texan. And if he had been born one month later he would have been a Canadian. . . . Yes, he told me about the old trapper Homesteader Bopy. He said he was a little boy when his parents died. And the old homesteader took him in. Said it was pretty tough at times. But Mr. Bopy gave him a pony when he was ten years old. He said he was in a country where there was lots of horses. So he said he got to breaking and handling colts. Said it was pretty hard to tell the old homesteader goodbye, but said he was old enough to go out into the world alone."

The beginning of the Bopy legend, apparently, had seeded early in James's mind and in a version that could be built upon as his imagination grew.

But as the wanderer, James was absolutely truthful. Close in time to Crouch's account is that of Ed Blackmore, a ranny of the Rocky Mountain country.[33]

> The summer of 1911, I planned to go to the Big Piney country of Wyoming. I heard they paid good wages for hay hands there. I wanted a little stake for the winter months ahead. I was at Orchard, Colorado, at the time, about 40 miles east of Greenley on the South Platte River. I had two good saddle horses and a good outfit, about everything a 'ranny hand' would use. I put my bed and grub on one horse and rode the other, and head out for Big Piney.

I was in no hurry, and in about two weeks I landed a job at a big hay-camp close to Big Piney. I stayed there about fifteen days. The Mosquitos and deer flies were so thick that I decided that I didn't like the country, so I decided to move on west to Vail, Oregon. My horses were in good shape, so I went across country at American Falls, Idaho. I crossed the Snake River there and went on west to Rupert, Idaho. I stopped there to get some grub and smoking tobacco and decided to stay all night. I put my horses in a livery stable and my bed in an empty stall.

I then went uptown and stopped at a pool hall. It was about 7 p.m. I got to talking to a man who looked like a stockman. I wanted to know how times were around there and how work was. I learned he was John Hagberry, who had a horse-camp south of there. He said he could use another man, and offered me a job helping trap wild horses. I thought I would give it a try.

The next morning we left town about 6:30. We headed south, crossed the Snake River, and traveled until about noon. John had a four-up on a good wagon and a pretty good load: grub, rope, wire, and other supplies. He stopped at a creek and watered and fed the horses. He said it was about 45 or 50 miles from Rupert to camp. We pulled into camp about seven that evening.

John's two brothers, Lew[34] and Ronald, and a fella named Bill James, were at camp. I was told who they were and I told them who I was. They had just finished building a new horse trap and were ready to start chasing horses. In a few days we got started.

There were five of us working together. After I had been there a couple of weeks and had been a good hand, willing to work hard, they got pretty friendly with me. I liked Bill because he seemed to do things the easy way. He was older than I was, so I did as he told me to. Bill and I rode together quite a lot and got acquainted a little.

Around camp, I noticed Bill drawing pictures of horses and women, and cowmen and animals. I picked up some of the drawings I liked and saved them. When we moved camp, I gathered up some more of them. Some were very good and some I thought were poor. I kept the sketches in my bed, next to the tarpaulin. I mailed a few drawings to my mother to keep for me.

Along about the first of October, we quit chasing horses and started to gather all the ones we already had caught. About the middle of November, Bill went to Montana for Thanksgiving and Christmas. I left my horses at the camp and went to Cheyenne, on the train. We were to come back by the first of February, 1912. It was a hard winter, lots of snow and cold as the North Pole.

When I got back to camp about February first, the Hagberry boys had moved the horses close to Snake River and were feeding them hay. Bill James came back about the first of March, 1912. Along in April, they shipped 400 head of horses to Miles City, Montana. Then we went back to chasing horses again. Near the middle of August, they quit chasing. Bill and I got our horses together and decided to trail them to Miles City and sell them. There was a good horse market there then.

Bill had five head of broke horses and I traded my two broke horses for ten head of unbroke horses to a cow outfit. I had another five head from the Hagberry boys—altogether fifteen head. Bill and I gathered another eighteen head, so we had thirty-three horses to trail for about five hundred miles. This is when I really got acquainted with Bill James.

We were about a month going to Montana, back past the Big Piney country, north of Three Forks, over the head of Powder River, and north and east of Miles City, trailing right down Powder River. We sold our horses, and had a good time for about a week. I sacked my saddle, rolled up my bed and caught a train for Cheyenne. Bill went on to Billings.

Will James was a wanderer, drifting wherever a wind or a whim indicated. In his early years in the saddle, he sauntered between Canada and Montana, then into Idaho, eventually drifting south. Some of the hearsay stories about him in Montana indicate that he was not esteemed as a rider and bronc-buster. Probably this is accurate information since James lacked experience. It could also account for his roaming—to learn and then go on to new territory where he would be accepted with better measure as a rider. But he also drifted because he loved seeing new country. If there is an essence of the spirit of Will James it is this lone cowboy aura in a classical land of space and silence and closeness to nature, "on top of a good feeling pony, the morning sun shining on fresh green sod, trees budding and millions of birds a singing everywhere" and with no room in his chest for anything except "what was all around, under, above, and ahead of me."

In his free, drifting world he learned of country critters and of range history from the golden memories of old-timers, some of which he presumed for his own heritage. When his first book, *Cowboys North and South,* was announced in the *Reno Evening Gazette,* the editor's request for a short biographical article brought this idealized note from James:[35]

My folks before me was range folks, my granddad's granddaddy made his own saddles, braided his own ropes, and worked the rawhide for his own chaps, there was no saddle shops then, cattle wasn't even branded, no shipping was done and a critter's hide was worth more than the beef she was packing underneath.

My folks seen them times and on till when the first railroad come west; it's right about then that branding irons was recorded quick, rustlers was hung and the cattle game growed till the longhorns lost their speed and gradually the white faced Hereford took hold, now they're in to stay the same as the cowboy which lots of people are wanting to put on the list of history and past.

I'm a descendant of the folks that's seen the cattle game from the start on till today, them generations before me leaves me the same as them, there's nothing but range blood in my veins and that's why I say that even though I did turn to writing and drawing I'm still all cowboy. I might wear a cap and Douglas shoes at times, I've even drank tea and talked over the radio, but I still roll my own and what I call my home is where I can hear the critters bellern, broncs a pawing the earth by my door and the good old cow ponies a waiting for the feel of the rein.

It was this sort of embroidery of a western heritage which was important to James. For he had himself said in his writing that unless a man was born in the West, he could never be capable of becoming a top hand.

And James's passion for the life of the cowboy in the West required this purity because he considered himself a top hand, the only sort, moreover, to justify writing of the cowboy life for which he considered himself its recognized defender and champion.

Doubtless, too, he changed his name when he announced to his Canadian family that he was crossing into the United States because his own had too much of an ethnic connotation. And the story of Bopy was a necessary and plausible excuse for his French accent.

James did know a smattering of English as a boy in eastern Canada, but apparently learned much more quite rapidly while in western Canada. Crouch recalls that he had a strong accent, and throughout his life, James's voice carried some foreign inflections.

As he perfected the story as told in *Lone Cowboy*, it surpassed, with a particular charm and beauty, merely being born in the West. He was the West's bosom son with a claim to a heritage that was a step above the legacy of one just western-born. It directed attention to him and made him at the core a special westerner.

By the time James was working the Nevada ranch country, he was a top ranch hand. And in that capacity, he could brag of a life that had sprung from the western soil as strong and as natural as sagebrush.

With the publication of *Lone Cowboy*, however, James left himself wide open. His biography, and most of his books, are conspiciously devoid of names, dates, and places. James excuses these omissions in his preface to *Lone Cowboy*:

> Here's a long story for you with no names in it to speak of . . . so you won't be bothered by the names of the creeks and the cow camps you might never heard of . . . and of riders you wouldn't know.

Perhaps it was shrewdness that caused James to take this approach. But others were not entirely convinced. J. Frank Dobie in his *Life and Literature of the Southwest* was sceptical when he wrote of *Lone Cowboy* being "without a date or a geographical location less generalized than the space between Canada and Mexico."

Ross Santee, also a writer and artist of cowboy lore and a contemporary of James, wrote this writer of his annoyance with James when he would talk about the "southern countries" that he worked. One time Santee remarked to James, "Goddamn it, states have names, an' when a cowboy works for an outfit the brand is known."

Perhaps James was reluctant to talk specifically and be *muy coyote*, because he did not want his early life easily pin-- pointed and perhaps facilitate the tracing of his past.

This seems likely, since, after James's first visit to his Canadian family in 1910, he made two other clandestine visits—one in 1925 and another more crucial one in 1934. Both visits were to erase any links with Ernest Dufault.

His return to his family in 1925 was primarily to inform confidentially his brother Auguste of what he had been doing. Apparently, James wanted to offset any possibility of Auguste learning about him through some casual look at a magazine which might have published a photo of him with his stories, and then making indiscreet inquiries.

James told Alice about the middle of that year that he would have to travel to New York to see Scribner's on business. Since he could not afford the expense for both of them to go, Alice would have to stay in Nevada.

James did not say when he might return. But Alice eventually became concerned that his stay seemed excessively long. She called Whitney Darrow who told her that Bill had left New York over a week before. She could not know, of course, that he had a home in Canada, or that he was there at that moment.

When James returned to Nevada he excused his lateness by saying that he had visited with friends in Montana. As it was obvious that he had spent extra money they could not afford, Alice became annoyed and reproached him, reminding him that he had decided she could not go to New York because they were short of money. She was upset, too, because he had not written her. James took the reprimand in silence.

But 1934 was the tombstone year for Ernest Dufault. Over the years, from 1907 to 1934, the Dufault family had accumulated many letters, telegrams, pictures, and drawings that James had sent to them. James knew that his mother worried about him, and while many of his letters and messages were brief, they at least indicated that he was well and happy. After the death of his father in 1926, James wrote only to his brother Auguste, who was providing a home for their mother. He expressed concern about their mother's failing health and instructed Auguste to do all that he could for her and to buy her a present from time to time and say it had come from Ernest. James promised Auguste that someday when his business affairs were in better order, he would make adjustments to Auguste for assuming his (James's) responsibility to their mother.

In a later letter, James told Auguste that he was developing a ranch and that their mother, Auguste, and his family should soon be able to come to Montana and join him.

For years all that James revealed about himself to Auguste was that he had business interests with a publishing company but nothing about being a writer. Doubtless, James feared that his family would find this fact too tempting for them to keep a family secret.

James's last visit to his Canadian family, in 1934, turned immediately into one of revulsion and severe anguish for his mother. At this time Will James and *Lone Cowboy* were nationally known. Even Europe enthusiastically received his writings. The Prince of Denmark was a particular fan and wrote James. He said he hoped some day to shake the hand of this famous westerner and expressed his delight with *Smoky* and *Lone Cowboy.*

With this acclaim and popularity, James became terrified that his true identity would become known and cause an unbearable scandal. So he demanded from Auguste and their mother all correspondence, pictures, drawings—*anything* that might link Will James to Ernest Dufault—and insisted they be destroyed.

His mother argued and pleaded with James not to destroy the mementoes of her Ernest. But James would not—could not—compromise. Finally, all correspondence and art were brought to him which he promptly burned. At the last moment, he allowed his mother to keep a studio picture of himself, but refused to write any message or signature on the picture. He instructed Auguste to keep it hidden.

Until the time of his father's death in 1926, James wrote to his family in French. Afterwards, he wrote to Auguste, and only in English. Their mother could not read or speak English and James instructed Auguste what to tell and not to tell her. James's letters, if handwritten, were signed with the initial *E*, and his typed letters spelled out his name, *Ernest*. Each letter instructed Auguste to destroy it after having been read, as it would be "a catastrophe if his true identity were known." It was sometime in the early thirties that James told Auguste in strictest confidence of his accomplishments under the pseudonym Will James.

James promised that someday he would have their mother, Auguste, and his family move to his Montana ranch. After *Lone Cowboy* had appeared with its wide acceptance, it was beyond hope that James would ever keep that promise if, that is, he had ever had that intention.

Regardless of *Lone Cowboy*, it would have been complicated enough for James suddenly to spring a different name, parents, sisters, brothers, and another life onto Alice and her family, Fred and Dolly, and other friends.

During the years following 1930, and particularly 1934, James deteriorated appreciably. Why? No one seemed to know or completely understand. Some said it was success and drinking that were ruining James. Others blamed Alice, saying she didn't try to understand him. But the true cause was the guilt motivated by the myth of *Lone Cowboy*.

Lone Cowboy had brought James's career to a pinnacle of notoriety and adulation from his public. With crowds and their attentions he was gay, witty, and very much in character with the cowboy artist and writer the public expected. While from the outside, James was riding the crest of the wave, inside he was drowning in dread of being "found out," and he could not call for help. Whenever he was alone with time to think of his fear and guilt, particularly with regard to his own family and Alice, his character diminished and he drank excessively. Alcohol became his anesthetic, the blessed relief of utter escape. And every time he drew a sober breath, the misery returned and drove him back to the bottle.

CHAPTER THIRTEEN

WHEN JAMES and Alice arrived home at Billings from Texas there was a new feeling between them. Collaborating together on *Lone Cowboy*, the first time either had shared deeply the mutual experience of working together on a book, they had transcended the agony of their lingering personal problems.

Alice believed she and James had weathered the growing pains not only of marriage, but of their individual selves. She felt useful, more mature, and needed. Through *Lone Cowboy* she now saw her husband as a complete individual, albeit unusual, but at least no longer a fragmented personality gleaned in small parts from his stories about himself.

And James, too, was different. He knew he had written a remarkable book, remarkable in that it personified a portraiture of a westerner, himself, that gilded the ideal of the American West cowboy.

Presumably, what doubts he may have had about publishing his partially fabricated life because of his secret in Canada were pushed back in his mind, and he was anxious to get on to new work.

His intentions were to stay close to the home ranch, and he dismissed the letters that had piled up requesting his presence at local civic clubs, historical societies and out-of-state rodeos. Through the local newspaper he expressed urgency in preparing articles and another book for his publishers. Moreover, he didn't want any visitors at his ranch for the summer regardless of who they were—celebrities or otherwise. His home, he told reporters, was his workshop, and being there without visitors was the only real relaxation he got while working. James also wanted peace and quiet to give support to the new harmony in his and Alice's life.

Also, by staying close to the ranch he had more time to be with Fred and Dolly and their son, whom James was allowed to name. He chose Clint, a name that had been a favorite with James and which undoubtedly was what he called himself when his parents addressed their letters to him as C. W. Jackson.

Clint was nine months old when James returned from Texas, and the "little fella," as James called him, gave him immense joy.

Alice had often felt that James's refusal to have children stemmed from a dislike of them. It was an erroneous assumption as Clint in his five years at the ranch would prove. While Clint was the favorite of James, his other nieces and nephews were remembered with books and gifts from their "Uncle Bill." And in New York, James's best lectures were given to children who eagerly listened to the famous cowboy.

To Clint, however, James gave all the attentions of a father. He bought western clothes for the boy and often took him for walks in the pasture to see the pet deer or the livestock.

A horse named Big Enough was especially purchased for Clint. After James perched Clint on the horse and showed him how to hold onto the saddlehorn, he would mount his own horse, and leading Big Enough, he and Clint would go for a ride together. Although Fred and Dolly rarely went to town, James encouraged them to take a day or weekend away from the ranch while he and Alice would care for the boy.

When Clint was about three years old James bought the boy a Shetland pony which he hauled to the ranch in the back of his maroon Hudson car, hobbled and standing on a large piece of canvas. Alice, Fred, and Dolly merely marveled at the accomplishment.

Clint, however, was not impressed and had repeatedly told his Uncle Bill that he didn't want to be a cowboy, that he preferred to play with his toy planes and trucks and wanted to drive a truck when he was grown.

James dismissed the idle talk and tried to put Clint on the pony. Clint screamed and kicked his legs when James tried to lift him. Dolly, to calm Clint's fears, said she would ride the pony first. Clint watched as his mother mounted, and was then immediately bucked off. Clint, obviously assured of his own instincts, turned away and went to the sandpile and his toys. (The pony was never ridden again. Alice says it was mean and ruled the other horses in the pasture. Clint, true to his childhood ambition, is today a professional truck driver and lives in Fernley, Nevada.)

Alice's mother and father came to live in Billings in 1930. Fred and his brother Paul, together with James, made arrangements to establish the father in a small carpentry shop business.

For one year, especially that summer and fall, there were happy times at the Rocking R. James had not ceased drinking, but it was accepted that he would now and then be "taking a holiday," as was the family's way of excusing his absence. The family gathered together each Sunday. Dolly, Alice, her mother, and the cook prepared Sunday dinner while James, Fred, and his father would go horseback riding or sit about and talk. Guests from Billings were often invited, usually the Earl Snook family, who had an art supply house in Billings where James bought most of his art needs.

One of the closest personal relationships that was to endure was between Alice's mother and James. She had considerable influence over him and loved him as another son. James was no less affectionate to her and always purchased gifts for her whether he was shopping in Billings, New York, or Hollywood. Whenever he presented her gifts, she would kiss him on the cheek and James would hug her. Once, Alice remembers him telling her, "You're the only mother I've ever had. Got to keep ya happy."

Mrs. Conradt frequently sided with James in his arguments with Alice. She would tell Alice that she must try to understand him and, above all, must never leave him.

By 1930 the ranch was in productive order. Fred had displayed the managerial sense that James had always credited him with. Winters were severe in Montana, but Fred and Dolly never faltered in caring for James's interest while he was in New York or Hollywood for the winter. During the initial development of the ranch Fred had waived his own salary when almost every penny James was earning was needed for the ranch. The usual employer-employee relationship didn't exist between James and Fred. Their relationship was much closer, with roots dating back to their cowboy days in Nevada. Fred did much more than was ever to be expected of a ranch manager. James was not ungrateful and, with Clint meaning so much to him, told Fred and Dolly that the boy would have all the education he wanted, and that James would foot the bill.

Wisely, James never attempted to interfere in the operations of the ranch. He did have certain ideas, mostly old-fashioned, which Fred did not counter in spite of the expenses involved. But in all aspects of making the ranch pay for itself, James allowed Fred a free hand. Whereas James found comfort in some of the old ways, Fred became excited with the newer developments in ranching and animal husbandry. He discussed with James his ideas for trying newer procedures, and James told him to go ahead as he wished. Fred started a program of crossbreeding their Herefords with a Scottish Highlander bull that was a gift to James from a Billings rancher, and he set aside experimental pasture areas for newer grass varieties. James took an interest in Fred's husbandry and horticultural ventures, but it was a token interest at best. Writing and drawing were his first obligations, and in person or in letters, he consistently told Fred to "take care of the ranch, old boy, and I'll try my darndest to bring home the bacon."

James and Alice stayed in Hollywood during the winter of 1930–31. James wrote feverishly, displaying again the enthusiasm that characterized his early writing days. He had completed at the ranch original sketches on the fly leaves for 250 special copies of *Lone Cowboy* and started the paintings for the Scribner Illustrated Classics edition of *Lone Cowboy*. The writing and illustrating of his latest book, *Big-Enough*, was accomplished that season in Hollywood and appeared serially in *Blue Book Magazine* in the fall of 1931 and concurrently in book form. Another anthology of James's short stories, consisting of selections taken from *Cowboys North and South* and *Drifting Cowboy*, was published that same year and entitled *Sun Up; Tales of the Cow Camps*. Whitney Darrow had selected the stories as a special book for the Junior Literary Guild.

Big-Enough is the story of a cowboy and a cowhorse born on the same day and "growed up together to where they were big enough—Big Enough for most anything." James dedicated the book to Clint.

James envisioned *Big-Enough* as another *Smoky*, and the *Saturday Review of Literature* was of the opinion that James's latest book was one of the few really great horse stories in the English language.[36] Actually, *Big-Enough* is not that good, nor does it have the originality and perennial appeal of *Smoky*. The book opens with interest and feeling and then tends to drift into a rambling narrative and a style that becomes more difficult to follow.

Big-Enough is nonetheless a pleasant story to read. But in rating the story, *Big-Enough* lacks the verity and marvelous empathy that is the hallmark of *Smoky* or *Lone Cowboy*. When James allows human characters to consistently predominate his narrative, they differ only slightly from thousands of other fictional characters who spoke their lines and were forgotten—and with them, the entire book. *Lone Cowboy* is an exception because James wrote with a very personal and moving emotion. It was an affirmation of love. His other novels lack personal truth. *Sand* is an example of this lameness when James has to use myths of the West and his personal prejudices as a crutch for his fictional tales. In particular, James amused his readers with shy cowboy episodes of the western fairy tale:

> and when she grabbed me by the arm and pulled me down right close by her I knew my heart lost many a beat.

Ross Santee, who frequently reviewed James's books, has noted that "James can get sentimental about a horse and it never bothers me, but when he writes about a girl, I always skip that piece. Anytime he gets away from the things he has lived and seen, and drags a woman into his pieces, they are apt to get pretty thin. But when James writes about the open range, I can always smell the sage.

Certainly James was far from the shy, unassuming cowboy that some of his stories describe. Anyone who worked the cow country as long as James stopped blushing many camp-fire talks ago. But James played up to one of the sentiments his eastern audiences enjoyed reading about. Maybe James didn't relish writing these exaggerations—he had expressed distaste for those passages—but he was also told that to sell books he had to give the public what it wanted.

Another finger-poking slant by James was with dudes, awkward characters asking the silliest questions and doing damn foolish actions around livestock. James actually detested those dudes who came West with highfalutin attitudes about themselves and their more civilized home back East. James never hesitated to describe them with reference to the back profile of a donkey. In a later book, *Home Ranch*, James has an eastern family annoying the hell out of an outfit which is trying to work its cattle on the range. The daughter, "a pretty fair looking young lady," is anxious to walk out into the range and see the nice cows. The round-up cook, hearing that, sets forth this bit of advice:

> "I sure wouldn't get in sight of the herd if I was you folks," he says. . . .
> "What would they do?" asks the daughter, disappointed.
> "They'd do enough to make you wish there was a tree close to climb up on."
> "You mean they'd charge a person?"
> "Yes, and catch up with it quick and scatter the carcass till there'd be no remains to be found," says the cook, half peeved at such ignorant questions.

Another time, the father of the young lady is wondering to

the cook why cowboys don't do any fishing. The cook tells him that there isn't much time for that. The dude answers, "Not much sport going on around here then, eh?"

The cook looked up from the batter he was mixing. "I don't know just what you call sport," he says, "but I think if you'd drop your rope on a mad cow while you're riding a spooky bronc, that you'd find plenty of excitement, and need a heap more skill in playing your line so's it won't get around you and cut you in two, than any skill needed to land a poor fish."

James's motives are apparent in his story-telling about dudes. They are silly at the outset, but in the end it is the cowboy, patient and silently grinning at these gazabos, who sets the dude straight on how a man acts in the West.

Occasionally, James employs the gun to move the action of his stories, although he abhorred its excessive use in western novels. He believed that the western story had been plagued with quick-triggered guns, consequently giving a gross misinterpretation of the West.

"For those run-of-the-mill, smoke-and-thunder sort of western novels," James said, "there is everything in it that will please them that don't know the west. . . .

"I don't object to guns, as long as they ain't pointed towards me, what I object at, by making that big fuss over 'em, is that so much that's good in the western life is covered up by 'em."[37]

James's contempt for these stories was no less than for the synthetic manufacturers who wrote them. B. M. Bower (Bertha Sinclair) was one of the few eastern writers James respected. "Bower," commented James, "is one of the mighty few western writers who can write a book, have a few shooting scrapes in it, and still have plenty of room to show a cowboy at work."[38]

James read infrequently and only themes telling about real cowboys at work preserved his patience. Even then he could be critical of a writer's approach to that theme and find picayune faults with the interpretation of facts. But James, in his way, was as guilty. He tended to be overly sentimental and described the cowboy as the paragon of true manhood, independence, and self-reliance.

Still, James's cowboys do not emerge the virtuous heroes seen in the cowboy movie or the typical western novel. He shook his pen and brought out the cowboy as a horseman, livestockman or drifter, who basically was lazy to any chore that took him off his horse and who could easily get himself into some sort of trouble. The ultra-good or the ultra-bad cowboy were extremes and were not worthy of attention by James.

He always prided himself on his fidelity in writing about the cowboy, and while his writing became repetitious and somewhat dramatized as he went on, he did show the manner of speaking, the casual daily life, and the livestock-centered interests of the working cowboy. He knew too, that by showing the cowboy as he really was he also debunked the western writers who hunted material "by going through the country on a Pullman, afraid to mix in the dust and get the facts." These were the exploiters, the victimizers of the real West.

Predominant in James's mind were Zane Grey and Clarence Mulford who were his popular contemporaries and whose novels were built around guns and "good guys" and "bad guys."

But to lionize James as the apostle of sensible writing about the cowboy and the West is fallacious. Another, Ross Santee, occupies a high step in the naturalistic school of cowboy writing. Moreover, Santee is rated above James by some who dwell on comparative studies of range and cowboy literature.

In any case, Will James was the greater favorite with the public, especially in the East. His books had the warm effect of a welcome letter from a friend, enhanced by his placing of a small drawing, after his introduction, of himself on a horse and holding the reins of another horse and saying, "Here's a gentle horse for you—climb on and follow me." As long as the public welcomed what he wrote, James was immune to what critics wished to spout about his books. The one exception, already mentioned, was criticism of his language and his grammar. He was proud of his cowboy vernacular.

Thus, in *Cowboys North andSouth*, James says in his preface:

> What I've wrote in this book is without the help of the dictionary or any course in story writing. I didn't want to dilute what I had to say with a lot of imported words that I couldn't handle. Good english is all right, but when I want to say *something* I believe in hitting straight to the point without fishing for decorated language . . .
>
> But as the editors and publishers seem to like my efforts the way I put 'em out, which is natural and un-diluted . . . makes me feel confident enough to give my pen full swing without picking up the slack.

Literary critics complimented James's first works as interesting in light of the language and the unusual hum of words and grammar which, if not academic, were at least honesty from the range land. For some critics, year in and year out reviewing of James's books became tiresome reading. One reviewer of *Three Mustangeers* stated: "Although not troublesome in *Smoky* and *Lone Cowboy*, Mr. James' ungrammatical style is becoming a bit weary. His latest book would be just as readable and fully as entertaining if a few of the more rudimentary rules of grammar were observed."[39]

It is doubtful that James's bad grammar was the reason for annoyance. Actually, his late stories were shallow and lacked stimulation, and the bad grammar sorely stood out.

Frank Scully, reflecting in his book, *Armour Bright*,[40] about his acquaintance with authors, says of James and others who write as he did: "These men with no formal education, learn to use language, not to be used by it."

James probably could not have recognized a noun from a verb, but his choice of action verbs bears truth to Scully's clever observation. James could use language. Slang, colloquialisms, similes, and range jargon were easy for him, and he used this speech with vivid and forceful emphasis. In describing the various sorts of bucking horses, James says:

And again there's the horse that keeps his brain a-working for some way to hang the rider's hide on the corral or anywhere it'll hang, and save his own hide doing it. He's crooked anyway you take him, and will put so much energy in his bucking that when he's up in the air all twisted up, he don't figure or care about the coming down. He'll make his cowboy shake hands with Saint Peter, and won't worry whether the ground is under on the side of him when he hits. When he falls, he falls hard, and the rider has little chance to get away. The pony seldom gets hurt, he's wise enough to look out for himself; what's on top of him is what he wants to get rid of, and he won't be on the square trying it.[41]

And when Smoky was mounted with the "feel of a strange hand" and threw his rider, "a few riders rushed up to find the cowboy setting up and shaking his head like trying to get back amongst the living."

In a less vibrant mood, but still tightly descriptive, James in the opening pages of *Smoky* describes the foal's first hours after birth:

His mammy was close by him, and at the first move the colt made she run her nose along his short neck and nickered. Smoky's head went up another two inches at the sound, and his first little answering nicker was heard. Of course a person would have had to listen mighty close to hear it, but then if you'd a watched his nostrils quivering you could tell that's just what he was trying to do.

James wrote his stories no differently than the way he told them aloud. His written thoughts divided themselves into sentences by context and natural pause, not by rules of grammar. He let his pen breathe and pause naturally to determine the punctuation.

James's writing, unless one wishes to be puritanical about it all, is actually a highly developed mode of expression. His best works are vivid and sincere and salty in understatement, satire, and hyperbole. Charles Twichell, son of Burton Twichell, recalls that a certain professor of English at Yale told James that he could write better than any pedant.

But if the purist is inclined to dissect James's English, he will find much to amuse himself; for example, the word *education* spelled *edducation, edication, eddication* and *education*. *Creature* James spells *crethure* and *creathure*. Often on the same page a word is spelled at least two different ways.

Whatever the grammatical rule, James most likely gave it a twist, and unhindered by most writing rules, expressed himself without inhibitions.

James was also a poet.

On some tattered drawings, signed 1914 and 1915 and in the possession of Mrs. James Riordan,[42] James sketched a gentleman attired in a tuxedo looking aghast at a man hanging from a tree. The verse reads:

A Man i know searched far an' wide a tryin' for to see
What sort of folks had roosted highest in his family tree.
He started in to climbin', but come shinnin' down with vim
With visions of his grandad a hangin' from a lim'.

Again on the lighter side of his poetic dabbling, James

relates his feelings about Hollywood when he was an extra in western movies.

Back to the Range

I've played the moving picture game
    And worked it good and hard
But it's too all fired tame
    For real cowpunchers, pard.
Them actor guys are tenderfeet
    That never saw the range,
And when they hit the saddle seat
    Their ridin's fierce an' strange.

They put us through a lot o' stunts
    That punchers never do
A fellow feels just like a dunce
    Before he gets half through
It's all a lot of honey-mush
    About some gal, you see
Twould make an honest puncher blush
    Sich goin's on to see

Because out on the range, you know,
    Around the chaparral
We never had no time to go
    Close-herdin' any gal.
They's too much rustlin' round for strays
    Or else a breakin' broncs
Or branding calves on roundup days
    For any such nonsense.

They ain't a cuss in all the bunch
    Kin cinch up a saddle right
Twould fetch a snort from a cowpunch
    Their togs is just a fright.
The other day I was most floored
    Whilst watching of the boss
For in a film he climbed aboard
    The Injun side of his haws.

I'm sick of all sich sights as those
     I'm quitting an' going' back there
Among a regular bunch that knows
     Range ridin' for fair.
I'll strike for my old stompin' ground
     Where range life is lived true
Where there's no greener around
   To tell me what to do.[43]

CHAPTER FOURTEEN

T HE WHIRLWIND stirred by James since being accepted as the popular interpreter of the cowboy in the West had created a great vortex. It had drawn to him all the good and bad things of life which, James had said, "all come at once."

By the spring of 1933 there had been enough happenings for him to run the gamut of his emotions. *Big-Enough* and *Sun Up* sold well, and *Lone Cowboy*, in its classic edition with seven color plates, was on a par with *Smoky* in popular appeal.

That same year one of his better novels, *Three Mustangeers*, was released. Issued the year before was the *Drifting Cowboy Series*, a five-volume set consisting of *Big-Enough, Lone Cowboy, Sand, Smoky*, and *Sun Up*.

Besides that, his status as a lecturer at art schools had by now bolstered his reputation as an artist.

Isabelle Johnson, a Billings artist, remembers when James

visited the Otis Institute at Los Angeles in 1930, while she was a student:

> I was surprised, as were the other students, at his knowledge of the structure of the horse. He made complete sketches of the horse in action; the colt in relation to the horse, the bony structure of the knee, its muscular structure and using anatomically correct terminology in each instance. His shy manner and quiet voice were in direct contrast to the positive lines flowing from his drawing arm and turning every joint and muscle of his subject into life.[44]

James's subtle humor, effective storytelling, and art demonstrations were lavishly reported, creating more demand for his appearance at lecture halls and autograph parties. While some lecture committees turned cool when it was suggested that a *cowboy* appear before their audiences, invariably they were pleased with James's presentations. They had to be prepared for some lack of the conventions, however. George Snell, James's attorney in Billings, invited him to give a talk at a Kiwanis meeting. With a sense of precaution, Snell asked James not to do any drinking until after the talk. "Don't worry, George," assured James. "But I do worry," Snell emphasized.

James arrived sober at the meeting just as it was being called to order. Instead of seating himself in the place reserved for him next to Snell, James sat on the opposite side of the long dinner table with his back to the rest of the members. When introduced, James calmly stood on his chair, then onto the table and delivered his talk.

"We were taken aback by James's behavior," says Snell, "but within minutes, with his dry humor and easy way of talking, he had won the club members' esteem and appreciation. You couldn't help liking the man."

By far James's greatest thrill was in the winter of 1932 when Paramount Studios purchased the movie rights to *Lone Cowboy*. And while in Hollywood later that summer advising on the scenario of *Lone Cowboy*, he was informed that Fox Studios had purchased *Smoky*.

These were the good things.

The bad things began with the death of Alice's father in July 1932, about a year after he and his wife moved to Billings.

His death shattered one of the most pleasant years on the James ranch. James himself admitted that that year was a time of fulfillment in having a mother and father to care about. James insisted on paying all of the funeral expenses and specifically emphasized that Alice's father have a new suit for burial. After the funeral, Alice accompanied her mother who wished to return to Reno. Alice told James she would have to stay for a few weeks at least, and James suggested she stay as long as necessary until her mother was comfortably readjusted.

In Alice's absence, James began the devastating habit of drinking while he wrote. His past addiction to alcohol, although excessive, was at least confined to places outside his studio. The death of Alice's father may have been the trigger, adding to the guilt he felt about the neglect of his own family and of Alice, and all part of a growing rottenness he may have felt about himself. Whatever the reason, drinking in his studio during work caused a calamitous turn in his life.

Fred and Dolly watched the developments during Alice's absence with painful apprehension. They didn't want to write her, knowing she was already in an emotional state herself, besides having to help her mother readjust. Fred was particularly torn and dreaded his sister's return if James did not stop his constant drinking; and torn too by silently watch-

ing a close friend destroy himself, knowing James would be-
rate him if he dared to suggest that he let up on his drinking.

When Alice returned to the Rocking R, Fred met her at the
railroad station and explained what had happened. Alice
listened in hopeless silence, offering little comment.

James was happy and affectionate when he greeted Alice
and immediately wanted a detailed report on her mother.

With Alice's return, he stopped drinking in his studio for a
few weeks, but started again soon afterwards. He told Alice
that "a little drink" helped his writing. Alice recalls she knew
then that this was a new wound, one that would never heal.

In the summer of 1933, James went alone to Hollywood in
conjunction with the adaptation of his autobiography to film.
Alice went to visit her mother and would join James later.
When she arrived after a few weeks, she was greeted by
James with a check for ten thousand dollars from Fox Studios
for the movie rights to *Smoky*.

Most of the *Smoky* film had been shot around Flagstaff,
Arizona. In preliminary discussions with the producers,
James suggested filming at the ranch of his benefactor, Ed
Springer, in New Mexico. But Fox finally settled their cam-
eras on the red rock country of northern Arizona.

The most impressive member of the *Smoky* cast, at least to
James, was the horse that played the part of his famous
equine. The horse's name was Rex, a veteran star of the silent
days when he was billed as King of the Wild Horses. At first,
James did not care for a black stallion playing the part, since
his story clearly said that Smoky was mouse color. He visited
the Jones Stable, where years before he had worked as a
stuntman and rider for silent westerns, to watch a demon-
stration of why Rex, black or otherwise, was ideal for the
picture. Rex was camera wise. His years of movie making had
proven him to be a reliable performer, wise to cues and work-

ing without restraints in front of the camera. Consequently, the studio did not have to go to additional expense to train another horse just to satisfy a color requirement differing from James's Smoky only by shades.

From director Eugene Forde's point of view, Rex was a natural because of his "tremendous personality," which was the essence of James's Smoky. Rex was dangerous, however, and at times, vicious. He would fight with little provocation, and this was what Forde wanted for the scenes where Smoky fights that "feeling of a strange land."

The horse, by the way, did fight all too convincingly. During the filming of the scene where Smoky fights two cowboys, the horse's temper was easily provoked by teasing and Rex fought viciously. Two of the scenario clerks began to scream as they were sure that the cowboys would be hurt. In the final editing of the picture, Forde had to cut the scene as it was "just too real," and he feared irate response from the public. After James saw Rex rehearse, he admitted to Forde that Rex did fit the role.[44]

Forde and the script writers had written narration scenes for James in the picture which would show James at his drawing board in his studio setting. His narration was to bridge time gaps in the sequences where Smoky matures from foal to yearling and then to full grown horse.

James was intoxicated the first time he faced the camera.

"We finally had to stop shooting," says Forde."He talked in a choppy rhythm, like a five-year-old reading from a school book. We assigned a speech coach for him, but he still read poorly. So we set up cue cards for him to read from, but he had difficulty even with this assistance. We knew he had been drinking, but he kept insisting he had not."

His status as a celebrity in Hollywood didn't do his drinking problem any good. With two of his books being filmed as major productions and with the strong cowboy and western theme that pervaded the lives and living styles of many actors, James was in a social whirl from the ranch estates of actors in the San Fernando Valley to producers' homes in Palm Springs.

Hollywood's attraction for James, with the heavy drinking parties and all-night horseback rides, infuriated Alice. There had been many embarrassments. Additionally, officials at Fox studios consulted with her concerning their apprehension about James's narration of the *Smoky* film. If James would not be able to perform, the script would require major revisions and would be costly to the studio.

Hoping to discourage his drinking, Alice invited her mother to Hollywood on the pretense of watching some of the studio shots of *Smoky* being filmed. For a few days, James stayed sober while his mother-in-law was present and completed a good part of his scenes. On the fourth evening, he failed to return from the studio.

The next night polo players from Santa Barbara brought James home virtually unconscious from drinking. Alice was beside herself. With the help of one of the polo players, Alice's mother put James to bed. He insisted that his "liquor jug" be put on the night table. Mrs. Conradt promised that she would, but emptied the bottle that was in James's hip pocket and filled it with tea. She locked the bedroom door and sat in a chair the entire night outside his bedroom.

In the early morning, James went into a tantrum, cursing Alice and her mother for the tea in his jug. The next day Alice pinpointed her frustrations about James to her mother, as she had tried to do for some years. Now her mother had seen James at his worst, but still she would not let Alice run him down. "He's a good man," she told Alice. "We've got to find a way to bring Bill out of this."

Later that day Alice confronted James with his actions, the obscene language he had used, and her mother's all-night vigil outside his door. It rocked him to utter disgust of himself and he cried openly. He swore he would never drink again and apologized profusely to his mother-in-law. A day later she returned to Reno with a promise from James that he would behave.

After she left, though, James again turned to liquor, prompting studio concern as to whether he could complete his scenes.

Alice, in a final attempt to have him sober for his remaining work before the camera, kept him from liquor by pleading with him to stay home one evening. But the next morning in the studio, James somehow managed to talk a studio hand into buying a bottle for him. When Alice came for him in his dressing room to take him to the shooting stage, the bottle was on his dresser empty, and he had a foolish grin on his face. Alice turned and walked out of the room and out of the studio. Forde and his producers finally lost hope of having James appear in the film as planned, and the final editing of his scenes allowed only a brief appearance in the released prints.

Victor Jory, the actor who played Clint, also received little aid or advice from James for character hints. "This was a hopeless task," Jory recounts. "He offered very few suggestions, and if forced to give an opinion of what my character might do or say, he would only nod his head, or say, 'maybe,' or perhaps just say nothing and look at me."

James never was pleased in the way *Smoky* appeared on the screen, although from an audience and critical standpoint, the filmed adaptation from the novel was successful.*

---

*Unfortunately, no print of this version of *Smoky* appears to have survived a studio warehouse fire. Perhaps one may be in private ownership.

Smoky was refilmed in 1946 and again in 1966. Those who have seen all versions agree that the first effort, especially because of James's appearance, was the best rendition of the story.

James's attitude is probably very typical of many authors whose original written work is treated differently by the hands of moviemakers.

If *Smoky* upset James, *Lone Cowboy* disgusted him entirely. It had no resemblance to his autobiography. But he had been forewarned that Paramount Studios was basing its story on the book and tailoring it for Jackie Cooper, then a juvenile star. *Smoky* received favorable reviews while *Lone Cowboy* was a disappointment to the critics. Both pictures were released nationally in 1934.

CHAPTER FIFTEEN

WHEN ALICE left the studio she went to their rented house, packed her belongings, and immediately returned to Reno with bitterness. She had resigned herself that James would do what he pleased and no one could reason with him. Moreover, she was convinced he would drink himself to death and neither advice nor pleading could change that fateful end. And to stay with him, she also felt, was wrecking her own emotional stability.

James remained in Hollywood that fall and made no attempt to correspond with Alice. In December James went to New York for a brief visit with Scribner's. A lecture tour had been arranged for him, but his previous commitments at the studio had cut into its itinerary. He told Scribner's to make new arrangements for the following year. From New York James went to Tucson, Arizona.

Alice, meanwhile, stayed in Reno unaware of James's location. Fred wrote her asking for James's whereabouts, but no one, not even anyone at Scribner's whom Alice had called, knew where he had gone.

In Tucson, James began another book. He wrote down about a third of his idea and then destroyed the manuscript. This was the first time he had destroyed anything he had written, or was unable to feel sufficient confidence in what he wrote.

February, March, and April passed without anyone hearing from him. On May 3, 1934, Fred received a telegram from James, asking Fred to come and get him since he was ill. Fred immediately left for Arizona and instructed Dolly to wire Alice that Bill was sick in Tucson. Both Fred and Alice arrived within hours of each other. Fred went to the apartment address listed on the telegram and was informed by an annoyed and irritated landlord that James was hospitalized following a heart reaction. Trouble with the police was also an unsettled matter. James and an alcoholic woman had gone on a spree which finally ended in James's apartment where they wrecked the furniture and fixtures. The police were called and the woman run out of town as an undesirable. Fred settled the damages bill with the landlord for $295.

When Alice visited James in the hospital he was in acute depression and cared neither to talk nor to see anyone. The doctor advised Alice that his condition was not serious, but his drinking would have to stop. After James recovered sufficiently to be out of bed, Alice had him committed to the Kimball Sanitarium at La Crescenta, California, and rented herself an apartment nearby.

While James was recuperating, evidence began to show that his financial affairs were muddled and that he was nearly broke. What had happened to most of the money he received from the studios for the sale of his books was a mystery. Fred accounted for some of the assets for the ranch operations, and James's attorney, George Snell, reported that James gave him a check to renew some of the Indian leases on Rocking R. When James was questioned about the whereabouts of almost six thousand dollars, he admitted spending much of it and lending some of it to cowboys. While Alice was aware that James did give money away easily, at other times fairly large amounts disappeared which he would not account for. In retrospect, Alice believes that James sent money to his family in Canada.

Alice telephoned Whitney Darrow at Scribner's to inform him of James's condition. Whitney came to Billings to confer with George Snell about James's affairs, since he was behind schedule in his writing for which advances from Scribner's had been made. Whitney agreed to advance additional money for James to pay his pressing bills, if James would begin working immediatley. And too, James's business affairs with Scribner's were now to be handled exclusively through Snell.

Whitney came to La Crescenta to discuss the proposed agreement. James concurred with the conditions, and also with particulars for the lecture tour. Whitney made it quite clear, however, that unless James took hold of himself in the next few months and stopped drinking, the tour would be cancelled.

James hardly recalled any of his actions when he was drunk. When Alice told him of his recent escapades with "girlfriend," James replied, "I can't believe it. Where the hell did I get the energy?"

The doctors advised James that he must quit drinking, as he seemed to express some sort of self-hate and anger when he drank. Moreover, James's black-outs—not remembering what he had done—could have serious consequences, if not for himself, then possibly for others.

The black-outs that would overtake James when he drank heavily twisted the skein of his character. He became nasty and destructive. Dolly remembers a meanness in him that resulted in his saying terrible things to those around him. "He was a different person entirely when he was drunk, and if it weren't because we knew Bill to be gentle and considerate except when he drank, I'm sure Fred would have left him long before he did. When Bill was like that, one could hardly believe how tolerant and gentle a man he really was."

The black-outs began in the early thirties, and actor Victor Jory, who played the lead role in *Smoky*, recalls an incident in the beginning stages:

> For instance, he would sit and tell me a story dealing with Montana. His conversation would go something like this: "I decided that I would ride over the northern hills to look for strays. This particular day I was riding a little buckskin named Copper. Well, sir, just as I got above—the—top—of—the—hi—ll . . . "
>
> At this point Mr. James's eyes would close, and as nearly as I could judge he had fallen asleep or had completely shut out the present situation. Perhaps five minutes later he would suddenly open his eyes and would begin to talk again, but on a completely different subject. It might go like this: "Well, sir, it was the biggest auction I ever attended—at least two or three hundred horse . . . "
>
> This type of conversation occurred twenty or thirty times during our acquaintance while filming *Smoky*.

The strange alchemy that alcohol wrought on James, a nastiness to others as a way of exculpating himself from his self-hate, had happened many times with Alice. It became a repetitious cycle, predictable as much as it seemed to be inevitable when James drank. The doctors, consequently, had advised Alice to stay with James, since he needed her very much at this point. Alice agreed to stay, at least until James's condition improved. But her marriage, she felt, could never be the same again. She could not bear the thought of another episode with one of his drinking bouts. She had experienced a great hurt, and in a letter to George Snell she wrote:

> I . . . realize that liquor was the cause of it all. I did what any woman would do for a man she cared for at the time, but to forget it all and start over again, I find at this time very hard to convince myself that it is my job to stand by him. I feel that he should be alone now and see how he will take it all when he's sober and looking things square in the face. I can't seem to fit myself in his surroundings without mistrusting him and being afraid he will drink again when I'm around him.

Alice stayed close while James was recuperatng. After a few weeks he was allowed to leave the sanitarium during the day and stay with Alice at her apartment. With amazing re-cuperative energies that were typical after his drinking sprees, James thrust himself completely into his writing and art. He was working on *Home Ranch* and the second volume of his *Uncle Bill* trilogy. The first *Uncle Bill* story appeared in 1932, a tale of a brother and sister from the East who spend their summers on a western ranch and are "edducated" by an old-timer in the lore of the West. Some years before, James made the promise to Alice that he would write a book for children who had always wanted to go West. *Uncle Bill* was a promise kept, and its popularity suggested another summer's visit by Kip and Scootie, with the title, *In the Saddle With Uncle Bill*.

James wrote and sketched each day so as to have his books ready for Scribner's by spring. Scribner's advances to James helped him clear some debts, but he still worried about the ranch which had been jeopardized by his heavy money losses the past year. Hopefully, James made efforts to sell another story to the studios, but his story ideas were only mildly received by various studio producers. Paramount hinted strong interest in another James book, but finally informed him, as did other studios, that they were not buying because of a business slump in productions.

In August, James told Alice that he felt well enough to go back to Montana and finish *Home Ranch*. Alice said that she would return to Reno. James wrote Fred and Dolly:

> I wish I was with you all because I'm sure tired of sticking around here, but it had to be so I could straighten things up and get in shape. I'm pretty well okay now but I'm sure weak from taking so much cleaning out medicine. I'm still taking some and seeing the doctor. Alice and me was over to that ranch in Santa Barbara a couple of weeks ago and I could hardly get on a horse. That sure surprised me, but the doctor says I'll come out of that soon as I begin taking enough exercise. It's a wonder to him that I can navigate at all after the ways he's treated me, but he said he had to do it, and he sure did. . . .
>
> The way it looks now, Alice is not coming back with me. I'm coming to the ranch alone. We've been gitting along fine since I got over my nervousness and after effects of the booze I had in my system, but we've agreed that we better stay apart some more, for a few months anyway and till we make double sure that we'd be happy together and for all time. No use fooling around, and we thought we could decide better and have a better chance to think things over while we're apart, while I'm at the ranch and my mind is normal and she's in Reno or somewhere she can think things over well.

His humor and teasing weren't diminished. He goes on in the letter:

I'm not so ornary anymore now. Alice and me ain't had a scrap since last evening and that wouldn't have happened only that we got our wires crossed. Alice answered the phone when the waitress Fred told me to sort of keep under my wing for him while he was gone called me up and wanted to use my wing again, then a while later a boy friend of Alice's called up and I answered the phone. I could tell by the sound of his voice that I wouldn't like the way his hair was parted and etc. Anyway that's how the one scrap started, but it wasn't so bad. It only lasted about ten hours. Had another little scrap today as a kind of chaser.

But laying all jokes aside, I'd like to hear from you buzzards, every damn one of you even if it's just a few lines or a finger print on a piece of toilet paper.

Bill

CHAPTER SIXTEEN

JAMES PROMISED that he now had the "booze"
out of his system. When he returned to the ranch he immediately set for himself a galloping pace night and day to finish
two books with numerous illustrations. Dolly wrote Alice
often, keeping her informed on James's health. Dolly felt sure
that James was truly curing himself since he hadn't even
taken a glass of beer. Alice replied that she hoped Dolly had
not misjudged James; but if he were really cured, he could be
proud that he did it alone and without sympathy or coddling.

After his work load eased, James wrote Alice an encouraging letter of progress about his health and his new books.
Alice's reply began a pleasant exchange of letters.

Snell watched James's progress closely and informed
Whitney Darrow of his marked improvement and apparent
sincerity in his desire to reform. On that notification,
Whitney started to arrange an extensive lecture tour for James
that coming fall and winter.

In a portion of a long and belated letter, James wrote to Burton Twichell in Connecticut expressing the new leaf he had turned for himself:

> I sure agree with you as to hitting for the land,[45] there's something about having a good hunk of land that makes "big money" seem like nothing but a lot of trouble. But I have some money to square up that hunk I have and square up with all my obligations. After that I sure plan on living on my land and from my cattle. Mixing my writing with my riding is my idea of fine and peaceful living, and reaching on and on for big and bigger money wont get no gray hairs in my head.

Tragically, however, the new horizon James had set aim for completely faded when, one afternoon, he came out of his studio drunk.

It happened the very day he had gone to town to mail the final chapter of *Home Ranch* to Scribner's. For the rest of the summer, James brooded about the ranch or stayed with friends in Billings. Liquor turned him again to near hibernation in his own inner sanctum.

Fred and Dolly, who had felt helpless anguish when they saw James drunk, wrote Alice telling of James's relapse. Alice wrote back that she was disappointed and doubted very much if her presence would have kept him from drinking.

James left the ranch that fall for his scheduled tour in the East. Before going to New York, he went home to Canada for the last time. As told earlier, this visit was one of sad family turmoil, when James insisted that all letters, pictures, and drawings identifying him as Ernest Dufault be destroyed.

Alice was living in Reno with her sister, Ann, at the beginning of 1935. She had not heard from James for half a year. Dolly had written her occasionally, but she too had not heard of James's whereabouts, although he would show up unexpectedly and then disappear again.

Neither Fred or Dolly offered any advice to James on his conduct. But Fred was deeply worried about the ranch, as it would be lost if James did not get his work to Scribner's. One time, deeply concerned, Fred pointed out to James that his drinking was jeopardizing the ranch, and also killing him. James listened quietly, but finally interrupted Fred by insisting that drinking helped him to concentrate.

When James left again, without notice, he left a note for Fred:

"Your sure a lucky feller," he wrote, "and that's what a feller gets for being good. I could maybe had the same if I'd been good. Dont worry about the ranch ever slipping away, handle it the same as you always did and things will be smooth again, and dont let anybody pester you with bills."

Fred was in a dilemma. He was too fond of James and had been with him too long to leave him. Nonetheless, he realized that the ranch could not exist unless James earned the funds to sustain it; and he wondered, in spite of James's note, if he were reliable any longer for that responsibility. Fred's bewilderment did not last long.

James returned about a week later with a woman. She entrenched herself as James's guardian and soon began to issue instructions to the cook as to what James should have to eat. She also gave advice to Fred on ranch matters. Fred told her to "go to hell." She suggested that Fred speak to James about their differences. Fred went to James and protested the woman's meddling. James threw his hands in the air with a gesture of non-interference and said, "Well, if that's the way she wants it . . ."

The next day, Fred, Dolly, and Clint moved into Billings and, within a week, were back in Reno. They were never to see James again.

The bad things continued to accumulate.

During one of James's fully soused sprees, he wrote out a bill of sale for the ranch for a thousand dollars. Alice was quickly notified by her own lawyer in Billings who advised her to come there as soon as possible.

The bill of sale was partially nullified, although the ranch stock and equipment had been sold by the buyer. Since James might not as easily be spared in the future if he did something similar again, drunk or otherwise, a legal separation was recommended to Alice. She was to receive the ranch property, but after all debts were paid she realized only three thousand dollars. James was to retain all rights to his published works.[46]

CHAPTER SEVENTEEN

BENEATH THE SURFACE of human life are the eternal mysteries of human nature. Will James, a modern Ulysses whose own odyssey had shown the gleam of the West to the East, became lost himself in a haunting pathos of that past. He followed his wanderlust almost in an endless dream of trying to find the peace and beautiful life rhythm he had enjoyed as a lone cowboy twenty-five years before. All he could find was the echo of his memory. When lost in an alcoholic stupor, his thoughts often came mumbling from his lips about the good old days—when he was just a broke cowboy, as free to follow the winds as a sagebrush tumbling along the desert and mountain foothills by the slightest hint of a breeze.

Success had cost James a tragic price. While it had made him a hero, as the public adores heroes, the astuteness of F. Scott Fitzgerald's "show me a hero and I will write you a tragedy" fits Will James with mold-like perfection. He had lost Alice, Fred, Dolly, and Clint for whom he had planned to do so much; and gone too was the Rocking R which represented his sentimental dream of the West. Worse, he lost his own self-respect by fictionalizing his life which betrayed both Alice and his family in Canada.

While James was usually aloof to any close friendship, Earl and Eleanor Snook, who conducted an artist's supply house in Billings, became an exception. From the moment James had moved to his ranch in Pryor he had drawn close to the Snooks, and often he would stay at their home in Billings when he had problems with Alice. During those years, they provided James with a cellar study for him to work in.

Soon after James's world had shattered beneath him, Earl found out his true identity through some letters to James from his brother Auguste. James swore Earl to lifetime secrecy regarding his true identity.

There was actually little left in Montana to hold James there. He became a drifter again: to New York only when necessary, to Hollywood which became his stomping grounds where he caroused with motion picture cowboys and stuntmen, or along the rodeo circuit. He never wrote Alice or Fred and severed all ties with the family he had so frequently proclaimed as the one he had never had.

Yet, there was an amazing tenacity in James to write. Whenever he was sick from the long flooding of his body with alcohol, he returned to the Snooks, and in the basement of their home he wrote and sketched. Earl Snook, meanwhile, had assumed guardianship over James. Whitney Darrow approached Earl to supervise James's responsibilities as Whitney could no longer depend on James to answer his mail relative to his books and affairs with Scribner's.

Reluctantly, Earl had at times committed James to the hospital, where he was at least forced to sober himself and finish what book he was currently writing.

When James returned to Billings in 1937, he was involved in a car accident. The Billings newspapers reported the story which was released over a national wire:

Cowboy Artist Ordered to Hospital
as Alcoholic

BILLINGS, MONT., (AP) Will James, cowboy artist and author, was ordered confined in the hospital for Inebriates at Warm Springs . . . by District Judge Guy C. Derry. A Jury of physicians found that the 40 [sic] year old writer . . . "is unsafe to be at large in the community due to his excessive drinking, which has affected his mind and health."

Earl's wife, Eleanor, remembered how pitiful it was to visit James, as he would beg for Earl to get him out. Earl could no longer visit and face James's pleading since he knew the only way to help James was to follow the doctor's advice and hold James at the hospital for his own sake. James even wrote to Whitney promising he would go immediately to work if Whitney would influence a discharge for James from the hospital.

By early 1938 he was released.Quiet, sullen, and reserved from the rebuffs, James retreated to his basement studio in the Snook home. Immediately he went to work on a book he had been writing during the past year before confinement. It was a rodeo story entitled *Flint Spears,* and was based on his article, "How Would You Like to Buck This Game," that was published in *American Magazine* in 1932. He also began working on the third volume of his Uncle Bill trilogy, *Look-See With Uncle Bill.*

Earl and Eleanor Snook were able to hold James to Montana for a year. Earl at that time had a ranch on the outskirts of Billings on a high bluff overlooking the Yellowstone River.

Often James went there to work and ride. He still drank but fear of confinement again checked him from excessiveness.

In 1939 he left for New York, but returned within a month. There was no particular reason for his trip other than apparently to get away for a time. *The Dark Horse* appeared this same year and the following year, 1940, *Horses I've Known*. These were his first major horse stories since his *Scorpion, A Good Bad Horse*, published in 1936. *Scorpion* wasn't in much competition with his other stories. It was somewhat far-- fetched as far as the human actors were concerned, but Scorpion's incorrigibility throughout the story allowed James some fine storytelling between two bronc busters. They banter words about and discuss the minute traits of Scorpion's bucking habits in the detailed lingo of their profession, all but forgotten today:

"I've got one started," says Pete. "Turned out as gentle as a frozen snake but he thawed out on me."

Unfortunately, James's excellent range terminology and descriptions of Scorpion's very different personality among horses have been forgotton as the rest of the book was unexceptional.

But in a straightforward way, *The Dark Horse* has a credible plot and good telling. And, *Horses I've Known* is a series of horse stories with excellent writing of James's experiences with horses. A story or two is a bit questionable, but over-all, the stories demonstrate James's marvelous understanding of horses. His love for them and his ability to read their behavior by noting only the slightest reflectional change in their eyes, the way they position their bodies for a certain action, or the cocking of their ears credit him with an absorbing understanding of horse nature.

James's storytelling in his last years is analyzed with mixed opinions by most reviewers. But his illustrating was definiteiy deteriorating. Whitney Darrow wrote to Earl Snook of Scribner's concern:

> Bill's illustrations were terrible . . . there is a feeling that he may not be able to come back in his illustrating. A book without his own illustrations would not amount to anything.

In the meantime, James had been accused by critics of being "washed up" because of his matrimonial troubles and his "illness." To the former James replied, "If I knew women like I know horses all my troubles would be over." And his illness he dismissed by saying, "I've always had a certain amount of work to do. I have done it. I'm going to keep on doing it in spite of hell and damnation."[47]

James held to his oath, and with amazing resiliency he sprang above the hell and damnation. He would tear loose with Death Valley Scotty in Hollywood, or with rodeo contestants in Calgary, Madison Square Garden, or Cheyenne. But he always returned to Billings to write.

For many years James had always believed that the great American novel would be written with a setting in the West. For only in the West, he felt, was there the strength for character study and setting to justify what was uniquely American in spirit. He even hinted that he might be the one to write the epic. Maybe James was boasting at the time, or playing with the news press. Nevertheless, he had an idea fostered as a bid to that singular achievement. It had swum in his mind for five years and he had titled his story *The Saga of The American Cowboy*, a sweeping chronicle of the cowboy told through three generations of westerners. Starting with the Texas trail drivers herding the cows through natural grass wilderness, the story evolved to the cowboy at the turn of the century and the devastation that wire fences brought to their lives when the range was closed, and with it, a way of life. Finally, the heritage of the man on horseback was to be continued to the riders of the 1940s . . . three generations of riders, and each named Bill. Each a man of specific energies that molded his own way of life in a western range tradition.

Moreover, James wanted to show graphically that the cowboy was not a man such as is made in the East and who was only an extension of British and European social customs. James's cowboys could not imitate the East, for only men of stagnant energy imitate. James's three generations of cowboys were to be men who stood high in their saddles and in a country "where there's mountains and badlands that no dam and irrigation will ever be able to take away from the cowboy, just as free and open as it ever was and will ever be that way."

This idea James discussed with an agent in Hollywood, who in turn had interested MGM Studios in a treatment of the story for motion picture possibilities. In 1940 the agent informed James of the studio's interest. James went to Hollywood and accepted a contract to write a preliminary treatment.

Almost immediately, procrastination edged his determination to write. Studio deadlines for phases of the story were met by James only through considerable urging by his agent. Periodically, James disappeared—no one knew where—but invariably returned with apologies and promises to finish the story. By 1941 studio officials finally abandoned the project and James began turning his story into a book.

Dick Dickson, who in association with Harry Sherman was producing pictures at the time, discussed with James a willingness to buy the film rights to his story once it was finished. To help speed the writing of the book, Dickson invited James to stay at Dickson's ranch in Palm Springs. There, in late 1941, James completed writing his *Saga of the American Cow-*

boy. He moved back to Hollywood and rented a house where he would sketch the illustrations. By then James had changed the book's title to *The American Cowboy*.

The illustrations arrived sporadically at the Scribner's office. Whitney Darrow became annoyed at the delays and asked Earl Snook to go to Hollywood and give James a push. The best Earl could do was press James to promise to finish what he had started. Whitney also instructed Earl to tell James that Scribner's could not allow any more advances, and that the only way James could get money from his publishers was to have them sell books. And to sell books, James had to write them.

Alice came to Hollywood that summer and through a studio agent obtained James's Irving Avenue address. She had not seen or heard from him in six years. As long as she was in Hollywood, she felt, it was proper for her to stop by and say hello. Alice was met at the door by a woman who announced herself as James's secretary and showed Alice into the living room. Five minutes later James appeared, neither cordial nor indignant. Alice was shocked at his appearance. He was thin and his cheeks were puffed. He walked stiff-legged and as if each step were painful for him. She had also noticed that when he came down the stairs from his room the wall was streaked with black smudge. She realized these were caused by James setting the palm of his hand on the wall and supporting himself when he descended the stairway. James and the house were dirty. He made no effort to promote a conversation and never asked about Alice's mother, Fred, Dolly, or Clint. He spoke about his latest book and how it was to be made into a motion picture. Alice could not believe he was the same man she had known. It was as if she were staring at a stranger. She became uneasy and forced an excuse to leave. James only raised his hand to her for a goodbye.

By July, James was finished with *American Cowboy*. Dickson urged him to return to the Palm Springs ranch to work on a scenario.

"It was hopeless," said Dickson. "For the past year he had been living on liquor. He wouldn't eat. It was difficult to communicate with him."

James was worn and tired after he completed *American Cowboy*. It had sapped even those energies that had always brought on his recuperations. And the hopes that *American Cowboy* would be his best work were unfilled. The novel had fallen dismally below what his mind had imagined. He bemoaned to Dickson that he had spoiled what could have been a great story.

On August 28, 1942, James collapsed in his home and was rushed to Hollywood Presbyterian Hospital. He died on September 3 at the age of fifty from alcoholic complications.

His last will had specified that he be cremated, and that his ashes be scattered. Earl Snook came to Hollywood to arrange for the final rites. Alice left for Hollywood immediately after hearing on the radio that James had died.

A ceremony was held at Forest Lawn in Hollywood. A small gathering of acquaintances paid their last respects to James while the King's Men, a then popular singing group, sang "Home on the Range." After the ceremony, Earl returned to Billings with James's ashes.

At two o'clock in the afternoon on September 23, a gathering of Billings friends assembled at the small rimrock studio house James had recently acquired, and while a eulogy was read, Will James's ashes were scattered from a plane while his last two horses, Pecos and Cortez, grazed—as always—outside the studio window.

The lone cowboy, whose self-advice was to "ride for the high points," both won and lost in a strange pattern of human life. Ironically, it all made for the legend that is Will

James today—the last cowboy legend, the creator of a final nostalgia for a time when horses, cattle, and men still dominated the western landscape.

AFTERWORD

THE WEST TODAY, compared to its romanticized past in James's time, is a diminished myth in the American psyche. World War II was the watershed for an old-fashioned and tranquil West. With the war's end there was a swarming migration westward. Millions of acres where horses and cattle had grazed became populated—and space itself was the West's greatest appeal. The intense movement is still going on and forever erasing the last vestiges of what was once the "Golden West."

The "Golden West" was Will James's West, where he recorded its last episodes of the working horseback rider. He did so in the same vein his childhood imagination had inherited the West's special feeling—with a sense of magic about it all, a curiosity, a glamour, and an atmosphere representing a special heritage.

And so he, too, was partly an image-maker, in the self-centered westerner's way of feeling, thinking, and believing about the West's moods and traditions. He conveyed the West to his readers passionately rather than intellectually, and on intimate terms.

Much like Rudyard Kipling's works, James's stories and illustrations attract the imagination of a child, and of the child in the adult who has not lost his ability to dream and imagine. To readers he gave the life of the man on horseback which rang with the purest note of being free. And as Kipling and his stories are British India's prototype, James is the West's. Each recorded the romantic interlude between the stark pioneer efforts and the lull after the romance has died.

But more needs to be said about James.

Some definite items about him have been left unsaid because I was unable to prove them. Also, certain individuals are still alive and the particular weight of these items would be embarrassing to them. Besides, they contribute little additional dimension to the already tragic last years of James's life.

I have also avoided any deep and searching judgments of James's relations with other people. What has thus far been told is based on or repeated from interviews conducted by the author. While a biography for perspective and balance may require deeper analysis, too often the failings of this attempt are apparent when that beam of attention is concentrated on over-playing the sensational and incongruous traits of the individual. Incongruity is in the make-up of all persons, but the famous and the creative are marked for their idiosyncrasies. Besides, it is only when one acquires a small amount of expertise in judging others that he also realizes how little qualified he truly is for making judgments, simply because the incongruous suddenly pops up in the individual.

All of which brings my thoughts immediately back to James. He was complex and held many secrets and guilts. His life, as were his writings, is a mixture of truth and fiction, of aspirations and frustrations, of deep moodiness, and of wild bursts of temperament. If these complicated the writing of this book, they certainly complicated his relations with other persons in his lifetime.

Yet, having scratched my way through the hardened shell with which James fortified himself, I can make some observations that have been neglected by others.

In the years following James's death, his personality and work have been criticized to unfair extremes. Critics have labeled him a phony and an alcoholic. Others had refused his friendship when he was drunk or obnoxious and did not hesitate to tell him what they thought of his poor manners. But James wasn't particularly fazed by those who refused to accept him as he was. Those close to him, however, had many times to overlook his almost arrogant sense of independence, his moodiness, and his impatience with those who tried to force their help his way. They learned early not to try and "figure Bill James out." What remained for Alice and his friends to offer was sympathy, patience, and tolerance—a compromise with themselves—simply because James was easy for them to like. He had an intrinsic quality about him that made one either like him in spite of his faults or dislike him completely.

During James's days of tramping, some of his fellow cowboys found immediate fault with him, but they still found room in their opinions for admiration. Oddly, both the admiration and the scorn sprang from a single trait of James's—his ability to tell stories. He told them with stylish believability. But some of the cowboys recognized James's tales as "fairly tall."

In the analysis of Will James's life and character, what has been overlooked most, simply because it was less conspicuous, is that he was also a poignant individual, made so by a devoted love of the western lands. More than anything else, he humbled himself to a country where, as he wrote, "a man can look farther and see less . . . of anything but land and sky." James was never religious, nor spoke of religion, but spacial and temporal domain gave him the feeling of God. At times, he came close to being maudlin when he saw the country being torn up for farms, homes, and roads. And he would reflect a sense of frustration at the impossibility of changing it.

One avenue toward some understanding of the James personality is the study of his denial of the cow country as it really was in his time. Frequently he boasted, verbally and in print, that he was not a cowboy of the 1922 variety. James was referring to the total change of the range country, the modern cowboy way of life, and to "dudes" of that era.

It is evident from James's books that he adored the West of the open range days when a man could ride from the Powder River in Oregon to the Powder River of Wyoming with never a fence in sight to force a detour. He liked to recall that there was a difference among the cowhands, the cowpunchers, and the buckaroos. They were men of similar molds and cattle-made, but divergent in their dress, their saddle equipment, their ways of stock handling, with each representing his own regional customs in the cow country.

Primarily, James describes himself as a rider of the open range days, before the range had been fenced, and before the time when a rider had to leave his horse to do any chores except branding.

No doubt vestiges of the open range days remained in parts of Nevada and Montana while James rode that country. But to the degree and the style described by James with his personal pronoun, it was unlikely. By the time he was born, let alone actually riding through the cow country, the range days of his romantic mind were over. And more, he grew up in the time when cowboys, in name and style, were becoming more of a myth painted with a broad brush by writers, scenarists for the silent motion picture art, and ham actors in Wild West shows. Real riders of the open range days were "stove up" by the time James was riding the country (from about 1910 to 1919). The nature of ranch and cattle work had been undergoing economic change and cowboys were pitching hay and learning about plowing and irrigating as range cow handling became less and less the basic economic principle of management. James's generation came after the era of the open range rider, in the twilight time when Charlie Russell lived his western experiences. Still, James seemingly had no trouble reminiscing with Russell about the "good old days" when they got together for a talk.

Nonetheless, it was the old West—the open range that lasted until about 1890 (1910 as the widest latitude)—that James loved. He talked and wrote about the country "as it was then," and much of James's wanderings about the country were very likely in search of this open range he harbored in his thoughts.

Often James exhibited active reminders of the old ways. While working for the Springer ranch in Santa Fe, he carried an iron cinch ring tied to his saddle strings and would use this iron cinch ring to run the CS brand on a calf. It was an old range custom, but it had died out in that part of the country some years before.

Dick Dickson, the film producer and collector of old western artifacts at his ranch in Palm Springs, stated that James hardly ever went horseback riding with him or his guests at ranch get-togethers. James preferred casually walking about the ranch to examine Dickson's collection. And on James's ranch in Montana, he exercised many of his desires to have the past brought back to life, or at least, to hold onto those ways that were being supplanted by newer techniques.

James was not completely overpowered by his sentimentality, and certainly not to the point of senility. It was, however, a powerful force within him, and sufficient to alter his personality at times and account for his enigmatic habits.

Such a mind delights in reverie, and James delighted in reverie about his lone cowboy days, when he rode the country from Canada to Mexico to "no place in particular—just drifting," on a good horse that he considered his "fifty-fifty partner," along with a pack horse that carried his home and his grub. Even as James was leading just a vestige of this way of life, progress was pulling it out from under him.

These thoughts of open range days and drifting only by the compass of his whim were most likely dreams that had filled James's mind as a boy in Canada. And his thoughts were long and reflective, as a painting fixed on a canvas. Reverie was both an inspiration to write and a mental retreat for James. The Rocking R—static, peaceful, isolated—was an escape for him where he could sit on the high bluffs and stare out into the big sky country. Only the Snooks and a few other close friends in Billings were aware of how the loss of the ranch had wrenched him.

He found a deep meaning in the land, an experience that he could never completely express in words. In a way, this is the real tragedy of Will James. His intense devotion does come through in his stories now and then, but not frequently enough to show the depth of that emotion.

However, James is not to be ignored for what he does express about the western landscape and cowboys, critters and cattle, horses and stockmen. And in this area, we reach a judgment of James that cannot be ignored—his talents which were offered to the public.

James's writings and style have been discussed, and it is sufficient to say here that *Cowboys North and South, Smoky, Lone Cowboy, All In The Day's Riding,* and particular selections from *Drifting Cowboy, Sun Up,* and *Cow Country* rank high in their portrayal of themes of the West. They were written without excessive frills and in a language refreshingly unaffected by formality or affectation. These writings have enough realism to be true as the earth itself, and enough touches of romanticism to allow expressions of the author's soul. They ring with the charm of another day in the West.

As an illustrator, particularly of the horse, James stands supreme. The horse, as the land itself, always inspired a surging emotion in him. He could fully express the power, symmetry, and beauty of the animal. By a gleam in its eye, the position of an ear, or the dilation of the nostrils, James vividly showed a horse's fear, rage, alertness, and no less powerful, the serene beauty of a horse in peaceful repose. He could not contort a horse into any position he was unable to photograph in his mind. Whether in pen and ink, brush and ink, stump and charcoal, or in oils, James's talent breathed life into his horses with lines lucid and honest. His ease and spontaneity in drawing were a great gift, and as the critics have noted: "For perfect expression of muscle-packed energy, James's broncs are inimitable"; "his horses seem to leap from the page and kick dirt all over you."

James was at his best with pen and ink, and his sketches are evocations of feeling and beauty. But he could become lost with oils. Charles Twichell (son of Burton Twichell) mentions in a letter to the author that a Yale art instructor stated James's oils lacked knowledge of design and composition. Specifically, the instructor pointed to the oil taken from *Smoky* of three horses fighting: "In the right foreground, flying away from the action, is a large jackrabbit which draws as much attention as the horses."

James, unlike the critic, was more concerned with an idea than a rule, and the critic could have selected another of James's oils to substantiate his opinion. The above oil has too much suggestive power of movement in the main horse action for the rabbit to draw away that attention. While some artistic illiteracy is evident in James's composition and design, it is hardly distracting. It is not of much consequence how James expresses himself in his art, so long as the idea fully conveys his own style and moods. But James cannot stand on the same plateau as Russell or Remington, who lately have been used by critics for unfair comparison. James, after all, was an illustrator—a very graphic illustrator. Russell and Remington were artists. Artists can illustrate, but illustrators cannot necessarily be artists. And while James did not handle his oils in the grander scale of Russell and Remington, his paintings were more than adequate for what James intended them. In this sense, James's art is highly personal in style, technique, and meaning, relating his emotions in singling out the dramatic point. Also, in spite of some critics' claim that illustrative works are not worthy of aesthetic considerations, James's illustrations, for the most part, can stand alone.

Still, critics and western artists toss about the idea as to whether or not James could have been a great painter. Perhaps he could have been. He did try, and possibly he would have relished recognition as an artist more than as a writer. Maybe success and commercialism, family problems, and his own guilts did build to a checkmate and cheat James and his public of his better talents in oils. In any case one has only his small output of oils with which to gauge whether or not he could have shown a brand of genius equal to Russell and Remington. The question is academic at best, but a certain thought of Dr. Samuel Johnson offers a form of evidence: "A man of genius has been seldom ruined but by himself."

NOTES

1. Ely *Record*, November 24, 1914.
2. Ibid.
3. *Lone Cowboy*, pp. 299–336.
4. Reporter's Transcript, *State of Nevada vs. Will R. James*, White Pine County, Nevada,1915.
5. Ely *Record*, April 30, 1915.
6. Ibid.
7. Now Mrs. Emerson King.
8. *Lone Cowboy*, p. 282.
9. Austin Russell, *C. M. R.: Charles M. Russell, Cowboy Artist* (New York: Twayne Publishers, 1957), p. 206.
10. *Lone Cowboy*, pp. 285–286.
11. On James's early illustrations he affixed the colophon "111" under his signature as a sign of his faith in the bond.
12. James relates, reliably, about Happy in *All in the Day's Riding*.
13. Bob Cormack, "Will James," *Denver Westerners Brand Book*, 1962.
14. *Sunset* magazine, December, 1924.
15. *Good Medicine: The Illustrated Letters of Charles M. Russell* (Garden City: Doubleday, 1929).
16. *The Times*, London, November 20, 1924.
17. New York *Times*, October 12, 1924.
18. *Editor to Author, The Letters of Maxwell E. Perkins* (New York: Charles Scribner's Sons, 1950).
19. *Bookman*, January, 1926.
20. *Outlook*, November 25, 1925.
21. New York *Times*, Book Section, October 10, 1926.
22. *Lone Cowboy*, p. 178.
23. *Horses I've Known*, p. 273.
24. Ibid.

25. Newspaper clipping in Billings Public Library, no date.

26. Both Alice and Dolly report that James abored this particular analogy and a visitor to the ranch was certian to hear the remark during conversation.

27. Newspaper clipping in Billings Public Library, no date.

28. New York *Evening Post,* May 4, 1929.

29. *The Review of Reviews,* October, 1939.

30. *Sixty Years of Best Sellers, 1895–1955* (New York: R. R. Bowker, 1956), p. 149.

31. The author had no success verifying these facts. Al Erwin, a cowboy who worked on ranches in the Saskatchewan and Alberta regions and served in the Royal Canadian Mounted Police during World War I, attests to detailed record-keeping by the force. In a letter to the author, he expressed doubt over the authenticity of the story.

32. A letter from John Crouch, sent to the author after the first edition of this book appeared.

33. This account was first published in the *Denver Westerner's Brand Book,* 1962, as part of an article on Will James by Bob Cormack.

34. Quite definitely the Lew Hackberry James rustled cattle with in eastern Nevada.

35. *Reno Evening Gazette,* October 26, 1924.

36. *Saturday Review of Literature,* December 5, 1931.

37. "Far West and Near West," in *Bookman,* August, 1928.

38. Ibid.

39. Boston *Transcript,* November, 1933.

40. Frank Scully, *In Armour Bright* (Philadelphia: Chilton Books, 1963), p. 168.

41. "Bucking Horses and Bucking Horse Riders," in *Cowboys North and South.*

42. At the time, the Riordans were ranch owners in eastern Nevada.

43. In the possession of the estate of Mrs. Eleanor Snook, Billings, Montana.

44. Letter to the author.

45. Twichell's last letter indicated that he wa buying a farm.

46. *James vs. James,* Billings Court House Records. Revealed in the proceedings were statements of James's earnings: in 1932 he received in excess of $25,000; he earned almost as much in each of the three previous years.

47. Billings *Gazette,* January 13, 1935.

SOURCES AND ACKNOWLEDGMENTS

IF IT WERE not for an error that Will James entered into his last will and testament, this book probably would not have been written. In paragraph five of his will, James bequeaths part of his estate

> unto Ernest Dufault . . . Ontario, Canada, he being the sole heir and survivor of my dear old friend, Old Beaupre [Bopy], who raised me and acted as a father to me.

As I was to learn, while contemplating writing an article on James, he entered his own name on his will, undoubtedly while under the influence of alcohol. The court could not act upon this paragraph of James's will without first finding Ernest Dufault who, technically, no longer existed. Forced by the will, James's brother, Auguste, related and proved, in depositions from Canada that Ernest and Will James were the same person, and that obviously James had meant to say

Auguste. One point is certain—even in death James desperately attempted to hide his true identity, to the point of using the Bopy fabrication with Auguste as Bopy's heir. If James had not erred, and had written Auguste's name instead of his own, he could have protected his *Lone Cowboy* image.

Earl Snook became involved in the estate dispute, and through him Alice first learned of the actual identity of her husband. Alice, the Snooks, the Conradts, and a few others legally involved held James's real identity secret.

Only by remote chance, while going through the courthouse records in Billings did I come upon the depositions, which in turn eased the restrictions of secrecy from some of the above people. In addition to the depositions of Auguste Dufault and his letters to me, James's prison record at the State Prison in Carson City (now transferred to the Special Collections Department at the University of Nevada library in Reno), the Ely *Times* (previously footnoted), and particularly the many letters and private papers of James now in the possession of the estate of Eleanor Snook* of Billings have all been instrumental in composing this story of James. The newspaper files on James in the Parmly Billings Library are a record of his ranch and of the local events that involved him. Also valuable is the Will James-Scribner's correspondence at the Princeton University Library.

Footnoting has been slight throughout the text and used only where the items are available. Otherwise, it is to the following persons that I express a deep and sincere gratitude. Each knew James mostly by the imprints he made on their lives while they were with him. Whence he came and where he went, his path was silently trod. But each of these persons has helped me connect the long trail—and the short side trails and the secret ones—that James made:

---

*Deceased

Especially Dolly Conradt of Reno for letters, pictures, and her recollections, which helped immensely toward establishing the continuity of James's life; especially, too, Bob Robertson* of Carson City, whose quick mind, backed by sound perspective, often helped me out of quandaries I habitually slipped into during the writing (to him I also am indebted for many leads to beneficial people and sources). Also Jeff Rice,* Winnemucca; Mrs. James Riordan,* Carson City; Pete Peterson,* Tonopah; Charles Keough,* Tonopah; Jane Atwater, Carson City; Mrs. Emerson King, Fallon; Fred Jackson,* Tonopah; Jack Connolly and Mr. and Mrs. Ed Slavin, all of Tonopah. And most of all my thanks go to Alice James (Mrs. John Ross), Reno, for letters and notes, for her reading of the book in manuscript form, and for the many hours she cheerfully granted me both through correspondence and in her home.

Also to: Curly Eagles,* Van Nuys, California; Clarence Jones,* North Hollywood; Victor Jory, Hollywood; Dick Dickson,* Palm Springs; Lee Rice, San Leandro; Eugene Forde,* Hollywood; Joe De Yong, Hollywood; Ben Steele, Bill Hagen, and George Snell, all of Billings, Montana; Ed Springer* of Cimarron, New Mexico, for letters and pictures; Ed Blackmore, Grand Junction, Colorado; Lloyd Garrison, Dawson Creek, British Columbia; Charles Twichell, New Haven, Connecticut, for releasing to me correspondence between his father (Burton Twichell) and Will James; Ross Santee;* Al Erwin, Palm Springs, California; John Crouch, Camino, California; and Harry Drackett, Reno, Nevada.

And to the following persons, my thanks for their interest in my interest: Dorothy Reading, Carmel, California; Mary Roderick, Carson City, Nevada; former Warden Jack Fogliani, Nevada State Prison; Lillia Pepper, Albert* and Nell Laird,

---

*Deceased

Carson City, Nevada; Parish of St. Nazaire de Acton, Quebec, Canada; General Services Administration, St. Louis, Missouri; Twentieth Century Fox Studios, Hollywood; *Sunset* magazine, Menlo Park, California; Jerry Armstrong, *Western Horseman*, Colorado Springs, Colorado. Barbara Mauseth, Nevada State Library; Stanley Adams, former Director of Readers Services of the Nevada State Library, for his suggestions, criticisms, and valuable reference assistance; Nancy Bowers, also of the Nevada State Library, who arranged many interlibrary loans for me; and Joseph Anderson, director of the Nevada State Library, who granted me the privacy of a writing room there.

Finally, but very especially, I want to thank Jean Taylor, my dearest critic and helper, who, as with past manuscripts of mine, has again offered her keen observations, suggestions, proofreading, and typing, all of which have made for a better book.

BOOKS BY WILL JAMES

Cowboys North and South (1924)
The Drifting Cowboy (1925)
Smoky, the Cowhorse (1926)
Cow Country (1927)
Sand (1929)
Lone Cowboy; My Life Story (1930)
Big-Enough (1931)
Sun Up; Tales of the Cow Camps (1931)
Uncle Bill, a Tale of Two Kids and a Cowboy (1932)
All in the Day's Riding (1933)
The Three Mustangeers (1933)
In the Saddle With Uncle Bill (1935)
Young Cowboy (1935)
Home Ranch (1935)
Scorpion, A Good Bad Horse (1936)
Cowboy in the Making (1937)
Look-See With Uncle Bill (1938)
The Will James Cowboy Book (1938)
Flint Spears, Cowboy Rodeo Contestant (1938)
The Dark Horse (1939)
Horses I've Known (1940)
My First Horse (1940)
The American Cowboy (1942)
Book of Cowboy Stories (1951)